ON
POLITICAL
EQUALITY

On
Political
Equality

ROBERT A. DAHL

Yale University Press
New Haven & London

323.5
D13o

Published with assistance from the Louis Stern Memorial Fund.

Copyright © 2006 by Yale University. All rights reserved.
This book may not be reproduced, in whole or in part, including
illustrations, in any form (beyond that copying
permitted by Sections 107 and 108 of the U.S. Copyright Law
and except by reviewers for the public press), without written
permission from the publishers.

Set in Adobe Garamond type by Keystone Typesetting, Inc.
Printed in the United States of America.

Library of Congress Cataloging-in-Publication Data
Dahl, Robert Alan, 1915–
On political equality / Robert A. Dahl.
p. cm.
Includes bibliographical references and index.
ISBN-13: 978-0-300-11607-6 (hardcover : alk. paper)
ISBN-10: 0-300-11607-1 (hardcover : alk. paper)
1. Democracy. 2. Equality. I. Title.
JC423.D2498 2006
323.5—dc22   2006009072

A catalogue record for this book is available from the
British Library.

The paper in this book meets the guidelines for permanence and
durability of the Committee on Production Guidelines for Book
Longevity of the Council on Library Resources.

10 9 8 7 6 5 4 3 2 1

To Ned, Charlotte, Angelica, and David

CONTENTS
•••

In this brief book I return to a subject—political equality—that has long concerned me and that I have often discussed in previous work. To provide a foundation for the later chapters, in Chapter 2 I draw freely from these writings. Readers who are familiar with them might therefore wish to move speedily through that chapter, or even skip it entirely, and move on to the rest of the book.

As I have emphasized in earlier work, the existence of political equality is a fundamental premise of democracy. Yet its meaning and its relation to democracy, and to the distribution of resources that a citizen can use to influence public decisions, are not, I think, well understood. Moreover, like the democratic ideal itself, and indeed like most ideals, certain basic aspects of human nature and human society prevent us from ever fully achieving complete political equality among the citizens of a democratic country. Yet in one of the most profound changes in human history, since the late eighteenth century democracy and political equality have greatly advanced around the world.

How can we understand this extraordinary change? I argue here that to explain it we must probe certain basic human qualities that drive human beings to action—in this case, actions that support movement toward political equality.

Yet these basic drives operate in a world that is increasingly different from that of earlier centuries, including the last. How hospitable to political equality is the world of the twenty-first century likely to be?

If we focus on the United States, the answer is unclear. In my final chapters I offer two radically different scenarios, one pessimistic, one hopeful; each of which, I believe, is highly plausible. In the first, powerful international and domestic forces push us toward an irreversible level of political inequality that so greatly impairs our present democratic institutions as to render the ideals of democracy and political equality virtually irrelevant. In the other and more hopeful scenario, a very basic and powerful human drive—the desire for well-being or happiness—fosters a cultural shift. An increasing awareness that the dominant culture of competitive consumerism does not lead to greater happiness gives way to a culture of citizenship that strongly encourages movement toward greater political equality among American citizens.

Which of these futures will prevail depends on the coming generations of American citizens.

ACKNOWLEDGMENTS

•••

In writing this small book I have been helped by a great many persons. The thoughtful comments of David Mayhew and Ian Shapiro on an early draft not only helped me to improve the text; they also encouraged me to continue working on a text that would undergo many changes. After reading that early draft, Bernt Hagtvet provided me with helpful comments and strongly urged its eventual publication. Stephen Smith saved me from some errors in the original draft. After considering and responding to the highly relevant and detailed suggestions of Jennifer Hochschild and Fred Greenstein, who read the revised version that I submitted to the Yale University Press, I decided to undertake a substantial change in the structure of my argument that, I believe, has made it considerably more coherent. Stephen Kaplan and Molly Lewis undertook the research for, and constructed early drafts of, all the figures and tables. My standing debt to Michael Coppedge has increased as a result of his generosity in once again providing the country rankings on which several of the figures are based. As

I point out in a footnote to the final chapter, I am deeply indebted to Robert Lane for his important contributions, both in his writing and in our conversations over many years, to my understanding of the sources of human happiness, on which I have drawn heavily in the final chapter. Finally, I want to thank John Donatich and Keith Condon at Yale University Press for their enthusiastic encouragement and their patience as I continued my revisions of the text, and Jeff Schier for his thoughtful and meticulous editing.

ON
POLITICAL
EQUALITY

CHAPTER I

Introduction

Throughout much of recorded history, an assertion that adult human beings are entitled to be treated as political equals would have been widely viewed by many as self-evident nonsense, and by rulers as a dangerous and subversive claim that they must suppress.

The expansion of democratic ideas and beliefs since the eighteenth century has all but converted that subversive claim into a commonplace—so much so that authoritarian rulers who wholly reject the claim in practice may publicly embrace it in their ideological pronouncements.

Yet even in democratic countries, as any citizen who carefully observes political realities can conclude, the gap between the goal of political equality and its actual achievement is huge. In some democratic countries, including the United States, the gap may be increasing and may even be in danger of reaching the point of irrelevancy.

Is the goal of political equality so far beyond our human limits that we should seek more easily attainable ends and ideals? Or are there changes within our limited human reach that would greatly reduce the gap between the ideal and our present reality?

To answer these questions fully would take us far beyond the confines of this brief book. I'm going to begin by assuming that the ideal of democracy presupposes that *political equality is desirable.* Consequently, if we believe in democracy as a goal or ideal, then implicitly we must view political equality as a *goal or ideal.* In several of my earlier works I have shown why these assumptions seem to me to be highly reasonable and provide us with goals sufficiently within our human reach to be considered as feasible and realistic.[1] In Chapter 2, in recapitulating my reasons for supporting these judgments I'll draw freely from these earlier works.

In the chapters that follow, I want to provide some further reflections on the relevance of political equality as a feasible and attainable goal. An important body of evidence is provided by the historical advance of "democratic" systems and the expansion of citizenship to include more and more adults. To help us understand the causes underlying this extraordinary and historically unprecedented advance toward political equality, in Chapter 4 I'll emphasize the importance of some widespread—even universal—*human drives.*

Yet if these basic human qualities and capacities provide us with reasons for upholding political equality as a feasible (even if not fully attainable) goal, we must also consider—as I shall do in Chapter 5—some fundamental aspects of human beings and human societies that impose *persistent barriers to political equality.*

If we then focus our attention on the future of political equality in the United States, we can readily envision the realistic possibility that *rising barriers will greatly increase political inequality among American citizens.* In Chapter 6, I'll explore this possible future.

In the final chapter, I'll describe an alternative and more hopeful future in which some basic human drives may produce a cultural shift that would lead to *a substantial reduction in the political inequalities that now prevail among American citizens.*

It is beyond my capacities to predict which of these—or other—possible futures will actually prevail. But I feel confident that the outcome can be strongly influenced by the individual and collective efforts and actions that we, and our successors, choose to undertake.

CHAPTER 2

Is Political Equality a Reasonable Goal?

If we make two assumptions, each of which hard to reject in reasonable and open public discourse, the case for political equality and democracy becomes extraordinarily powerful. The first is the moral judgment that all human beings are of equal intrinsic worth, that no person is intrinsically superior to another, and that the good or interests of each person must be given equal consideration.[1] Let me call this the assumption of intrinsic equality.

Even if we accept this moral judgment, the deeply troublesome question immediately arises: who or what group is best qualified to decide what the good or interests of a person really are? Clearly the answer will vary depending on the situation, the kinds of decisions, and the persons involved. But if we restrict our focus to the government of a state, then it seems to me that the safest and most prudent assumption would run something like this: Among adults no persons are so definitely better qualified than others to govern that they should be entrusted with complete and final authority over the government of the state.

Although we might reasonably add refinements and qualifications to this prudential judgment, for at least three reasons it is difficult to see how any substantially different proposition could be supported. First, Acton's famous and oft quoted proposition appears to express a fundamental truth about human beings: power corrupts, and absolute power corrupts absolutely. Whatever the intentions of rulers may be at the outset of their rule, any commitment they may have to serving "the public good" is likely to be transformed in time into an identification of "the public good" with the maintenance of the their own powers and privileges. Second, just as free discussion and controversy are, as John Stuart Mill famously argued, essential to the pursuit of truth—or, if you prefer, to reasonably justifiable judgments—a government unchecked by citizens who are free to discuss and oppose the policies of their leaders is more likely to blunder, sometimes disastrously, as modern authoritarian regimes have amply demonstrated.[2] Finally, consider the most crucial historical cases in which substantial numbers of persons were denied equal citizenship: does anyone really believe today that when the working classes, women, and racial and ethnic minorities were excluded from political participation, their interests were adequately considered and protected by those who were privileged to govern them?

I do not mean to say that the reasons I have given were in

the minds of the persons who brought about greater political equality. I am simply saying that moral and prudential judgments offer strong support for political equality as a desirable and reasonable goal or ideal.

POLITICAL EQUALITY AND DEMOCRACY

If we conclude that political equality is desirable in governing a state (though not necessarily in all other human associations), how may it be achieved? It almost goes without saying that the only political system for governing a state that derives its legitimacy and its political institutions from the idea of political equality is a democracy. What political institutions are necessary in order for a political system to qualify as a democracy? And why these institutions?

IDEAL VS. ACTUAL

We can't answer these questions satisfactorily, I believe, without a concept of an ideal democracy. For the same reasons that Aristotle found it useful to describe his three ideal constitutions in order to classify actual systems, a description of an ideal democracy provides a model against which to compare various actual systems. Unless we have a conception of the ideal against which to compare the actual, our reasoning will be circular or purely arbitrary: e.g., "the United States, Britain, France, and Norway are all democracies;

therefore, the political institutions they all have in common must be the basic institutions that are necessary to democracy; therefore, since these countries possess these institutions, they must be democracies."

We need to keep in mind that a description of an "ideal" system can serve two different but entirely compatible purposes. One is to assist in empirical or scientific theory. The other is to help us make moral judgments by providing an ideal end or goal. These are often confused, though an "ideal" in the first sense does not necessarily imply an "ideal" in the other.

In empirical theory the function of an ideal system is to describe the characteristics or operation of that system under a set of perfect (ideal) conditions. Galileo inferred the rate at which an object would fall in a vacuum—i.e., under ideal conditions—by measuring the speed of a marble rolling down an inclined plane. Obviously he did not and could not measure its rate of fall in a vacuum. Yet his law of falling bodies remains valid today. It is not uncommon in physics to formulate hypotheses concerning the behavior of an object or force under ideal conditions that cannot be perfectly attained in actual experiments but that can be satisfactorily approximated. In a similar spirit, when the German sociologist Max Weber described "three pure types of legitimate authority" he commented that "the usefulness of the above classification can only be judged by its results in promoting systematic analysis . . . [N]one of these three ideal types . . . is usually to be found in historical cases in 'pure' form."[3]

An ideal in the second sense is understood as a desirable goal, one probably not perfectly achievable in practice, but a standard to which we ought to aspire, and against which we can measure the good or value of what has been achieved, what actually exists.

A definition and description of democracy may be intended to serve only the first purpose; or it may serve the second as well. As an aid to empirical theory, a conception of democracy may come not from an advocate but from a critic for whom even the ideal is unsatisfactory, or simply irrelevant to human experience because of the enormous gap between the goal and any possibility of a satisfactory approximation.

IDEAL DEMOCRACY

Although an ideal democracy might be portrayed in many ways, a useful starting point is the etymological origins of the term: *demos* + *kratia,* rule by "the people." In order to leave open the question of just which "people" are provided with full political equality, instead of "the people" let me briefly use the more neutral term "demos."

At a minimum an ideal democracy would, I believe, require these features:

- Effective participation. Before a policy is adopted by the association, all the members of the demos must have equal and effective opportunities for making known to other members their views about what the policy should be.
- Equality in voting. When the moment arrives at which the decision will finally be made, every member must have an equal and effective opportunity to vote, and all votes must be counted as equal.
- Gaining enlightened understanding. Within a reasonable amount of time, each member would have equal and effective opportunities for learning about the relevant alternative policies and their likely consequences.
- Final control of the agenda. The demos would have the exclusive opportunity to decide how (and if) its members chose which matters are to be placed on the agenda. Thus the democratic process required by the three preceding features would never be closed. The policies of the association would always be open to change by the demos, if its members chose to do so.
- Inclusion. Every member of the demos would be entitled to participate in the ways just described: effective participation, equality in voting, seeking an enlightened understanding of the issues, and exercising final control over the agenda.

- Fundamental rights. Each of the necessary features of an ideal democracy prescribes a right that is itself a necessary part of an ideal democratic order: a right to participate, a right to have one's vote counted equally with the votes of others, a right to search for the knowledge necessary in order to understand the issue on the agenda, and a right to participate on an equal footing with one's fellow citizens in exercising final control over the agenda. Democracy consists, then, not only of political processes. It is also necessarily a system of fundamental rights.

ACTUAL DEMOCRATIC SYSTEMS

Political philosophers from Aristotle to Rousseau and later have generally insisted that no actual political system is likely to meet fully the requirements of the ideal. Although the political institutions of actual democracies may be *necessary* in order for a political system to attain a relatively high level of democracy, they may not be, indeed almost certainly will not be, *sufficient* to achieve anything like perfect or ideal democracy. Yet the institutions amount to a large step toward the ideal, as presumably they did in Athens when citizens, leaders, and political philosophers named their system a democracy—i.e., an actual if not ideal democracy—or in the United States when Tocqueville, like most others in America and elsewhere, unhesitatingly called it a democracy.

If a unit is small in numbers and area, the political institutions of assembly democracy could readily be seen as fulfilling the requirements for a "government by the people." The citizens would be free to learn as much as they could about the proposals that are to come before them. They could discuss policies and proposals with their fellow citizens, seek out information from members they regard as better informed, and consult written or other sources. They could meet at a convenient place—Pnyx Hill in Athens, the Forum in Rome, the Palazzo Ducale in Venice, the town hall in a New England village. There, under the guidance of a neutral moderator, within reasonable time limits they could discuss, debate, amend, propose. Finally, they could cast their votes, all votes being counted equal, with the votes of a majority prevailing.

It is easy to see, then, why assembly democracy is sometimes thought to be much closer to the ideal than a representative system could possibly be, and why the most ardent advocates of assembly democracy sometimes insist, like Rousseau in the Social Contract, that the term *representative democracy* is self-contradictory. Yet views like these have failed to win many converts.

THE POLITICAL INSTITUTIONS OF
REPRESENTATIVE DEMOCRACY

Throughout the nineteenth and twentieth centuries in Europe and the English-speaking countries a set of political institutions needed for democratic representative governments evolved that, taken as a whole, was entirely new in human history.[4] Despite important differences in constitutional structures, these basic political institutions are similar in their broad outlines. The most important are:

- Important government decisions and policies are directly or indirectly adopted by, or accountable to, officials who are chosen in popular elections.
- Citizens are entitled to participate freely in fair and reasonably frequent elections in which coercion is uncommon.
- Citizens are entitled to run for and serve in elective offices, though requirements as to age and place of residence may be imposed.
- Citizens may express themselves publicly over a broad range of politically relevant subjects, without danger of severe punishment.
- All citizens are entitled to seek out independent sources of information from other citizens, newspapers, and many other sources; moreover, sources of information not under the control of the government or any single group

actually exist and are effectively protected by law in their expression.

- In full contrast to the prevailing view in earlier democracies and republics that political "factions" were a danger to be avoided, both theory and practice came to insist that in order for citizens to achieve their various rights they must possess a further right to form and participate in relatively independent associations and organizations, including independent political parties and interest groups.

Political institutions like these developed in different countries under various political and historical circumstances, and they were not necessarily fostered only by democratic impulses. Yet it would become increasingly apparent that they were necessary institutions for achieving a satisfactory level of democracy in a political unit, like a country, that was too large for assembly democracy.

The relation between the institutions of actual (large-scale) democracy and the requirements of an ideal democracy can be summarized thus:

In a unit as large as a country, these political institutions are necessary:	in order to satisfy these criteria of ideal democracy:
1. Elected representatives	Effective participation
	Control of the agenda
2. Free, fair, and frequent elections	Voting equality
	Effective participation
3. Freedom of expression	Effective participation
	Enlightened understanding
	Control of the agenda
4. Alternative sources of information	Effective participation
	Enlightened understanding
	Control of the agenda
5. Associational autonomy	Effective participation
	Enlightened understanding
	Control of the agenda
6. Inclusion of all members of the demos	Effective participation
	Voting equality
	Enlightened understanding
	Control of the agenda

LEGITIMATE LIMITS ON THE POWER OF THE DEMOS

If citizens disagree on policies, whose views should prevail? The standard answer in democratic systems is that the decision must follow the will of the majority of citizens, or in representative systems, the majority of their representatives in the legislative body. Because the principle of majority rule and its justification have been the subject of careful and, I believe, convincing analyses from John Locke to the present day, I shall not undertake to justify majority rule except to say that no other rule appears to be consistent with the assumption that all citizens are entitled to be treated as political equals. Although majority rule is not without problems, these are not at issue here.[5]

To return now to our question: If we assume that membership in the demos and the necessary political institutions have been satisfactorily established, what *limits* may properly be placed on the authority of the demos to enact laws, and more concretely, on the authority of a *majority* of the members of the demos?

NECESSARY DEMOCRATIC RIGHTS

If we believe in the desirability and feasibility of representative democracy for large-scale political systems, and if the institutions I have just mentioned, together with their requisite rights, are necessary for representative democracy, then it follows that actions that would significantly weaken or even destroy these rights cannot be legitimate and may properly be placed outside the legal and constitutional authority of majorities. Although a thorough examination of the issue would take us further than I wish to go here, as a matter of straightforward logic it seems obvious that *the fundamental rights necessary to democracy itself* cannot legitimately be infringed by majorities whose actions are justified only by the principle of political equality. Simply put, if we assume that:

1. Achieving political equality is a desirable and feasible goal.
2. Majority rule is justified only as a means of achieving political equality.
3. A democratic political system is a necessary (though not sufficient) condition for achieving political equality.
4. And certain rights are necessary (though not sufficient) for fully achieving a democratic political system.

Then it follows that:

- To deny or infringe on these necessary rights would harm a democratic political system.
- By harming a democratic system, these denials or infringements on necessary rights would harm political equality.
- If majority rule is justified only as a means of achieving political equality (assumption 2, above), the principle of majority rule cannot reasonably justify actions that inflict harm on rights necessary to a democratic system.

It would not be inconsistent with democratic beliefs, then, to impose limits on the authority of a majority to undertake actions that would destroy an institution like freedom of speech that is necessary if a democratic system is to exist. This is the intent, for example, of a Bill of Rights embedded in a constitution that cannot be altered by ordinary majorities of 50 percent plus one, but instead requires that amendments must be passed by *supermajorities.*

Logically, of course, even the members of the requisite supermajority required for constitutional change could not logically believe both in the desirability democracy and at the same time support a constitutional amendment that would severely impair or destroy one of its requisites, such as freedom of speech, free and fair elections, and others listed above.

Here we pass over the threshold from *ought* to *is.* In the world of empirical reality, if a preponderant majority of active citizens in a democratic country persistently believe that a right necessary to democracy is undesirable and should be sharply limited or abolished, then that right is very likely to be curtailed. Even an independent judiciary would be unable to stem a strong tide running steadily against democratic rights. When a demos ceases to believe that the rights necessary to democracy are desirable, their democracy will soon become an oligarchy or a tyranny.

There is, however, another and more insidious route from democracy to oligarchy. Even if most members of the demos continue to *believe* in the desirability of these fundamental rights, they may fail to undertake the *political actions* that would be necessary in order to protect and preserve those rights from infringements imposed by political leaders who possess greater resources for gaining their own political ends.

IS POLITICAL EQUALITY A FEASIBLE GOAL?

These observations pose a fundamental and troubling question. Even if we believe that political equality is a highly desirable goal, and that this goal is best achieved in a democratic political system, is the goal really achievable, even in a democratic system? Or do some fundamental aspects of human beings and human society present barriers to political equality so high that for all practical purposes the goal is and will remain so distant that we should abandon efforts to achieve it?

The United States provides telling examples of the huge gap between the rhetoric and reality of political equality. In the second paragraph of a document that is otherwise a rather tedious listing of the "repeated injuries and usurpations" inflicted by the king of Great Britain, we encounter the famous assertion of a supposedly self-evident truth, that all men are created equal. The authors of the American Declaration of Independence and the fifty-five delegates to the Second Continental Congress who voted to adopt it in July 1776, were, of course, all men, none of whom had the slightest intention of extending the suffrage or many other basic political and civil rights to women, who, in legal contemplation, were essentially the property of their fathers or husbands.

"Of women," Rogers Smith writes in his masterful work on American citizenship, "the Constitution said nothing directly. It did, however, use masculine pronouns thirty times describing U.S. Representatives, Senators, the Vice-President and the President . . . The salient fact . . . was the Constitution left intact the state constitutions that denied women the franchise and other legal and political privileges."[6]

Nor did the worthy supporters of the Declaration intend to include slaves or, for that matter, free persons of African origin, who were a substantial fraction of the population in almost all the colonies that now claimed the right to become independent self-governing republics.[7] The principal author of the Declaration, Thomas Jefferson, owned several hundred slaves, none of whom he freed during his life; and he freed only five on his death.[8] It was not until more than four score and seven years later (to borrow a poetic phrase from Lincoln's Gettysburg Address) that slavery was legally abolished in the United States by force of arms and constitutional enactment. And it took yet another century before the rights of African Americans to participate in political life began to be effectively enforced in the American South. Now, two generations later, Americans white and black still bear the deep wounds that slavery and its aftermath inflicted on human equality, freedom, dignity, and respect.

Our noble Declaration also silently excluded the people who for some thousands of years had inhabited the lands that Europeans colonized and came to occupy. We are all, I think, familiar with the story of how the settlers denied homes, land, place, freedom, dignity, and humanity to these earlier peoples of America, whose descendants even today continue to suffer from the effects of their treatment throughout several centuries when their most elementary claims to legal, economic, and political—not to say social— standing as equal human beings were rejected, often by violence, a lengthy period followed more recently by neglect and indifference.

All this in a country that visitors from Europe like Tocqueville portrayed, quite correctly, I think, as displaying a passion for equality stronger than they had ever observed elsewhere.

It would be easy to provide endless examples from other democratic countries. Many Europeans would probably agree that over many centuries the people of one of the most advanced democratic countries in the world, Britain, have been concerned more passionately than in any other western European country with maintaining social inequalities in the form of differences in class and status, which in turn played out in many ways, notably in higher education, the admirable British Civil Service, the professions, including law and justice, and business. Until only a few years ago, unlike any other democratic country in the world, Britain maintained the astonishing anachronism of an upper house in its national parliament consisting overwhelmingly of hereditary peers.

The historical gap between the public rhetoric and reality of political equality is by no means unique to the United States and Britain. In many "democratic" countries, large parts of the adult male population were excluded from the suffrage until late in the nineteenth century, or even until the twentieth century. And only two "democratic" countries—New Zealand and Australia—had extended the suffrage to women in national elections before the 1920s. In France and Belgium, women did not gain the suffrage in national elections until after the Second World War. In Switzerland, where universal male suffrage was established for males in 1848, women were not guaranteed the right to vote until 1971.

So much for the rhetorical commitment to political equality so often asserted by leaders and by many citizens—male citizens—in "democratic" countries.

THE GROWTH OF POLITICAL EQUALITY

Despite the obvious fact that equality has often been denied in practice in many places, remarkably over the past several centuries many claims to equality, including political equality, have come to be strongly reinforced by institutions, practices, and behavior. Although this monumental historical movement is in some respects worldwide, it has been most conspicuous, perhaps, in democratic countries like Britain, France, the United States, the Scandinavian countries, Holland, and many others.

In the opening pages of the first volume of *Democracy in America* Tocqueville pointed to the inexorable increase in the equality of conditions among his French countrymen "at intervals of fifty years, beginning with the eleventh century." Nor was this revolution taking place only in his own country: "Whithersoever we turn our eyes," he wrote, "we shall witness the same continual revolution throughout the whole of Christendom."

"The gradual development of the equality of conditions," he goes on to say, "is . . . a providential fact, and it possesses all the characteristics of a Divine decree: it is universal, it is durable, it constantly eludes all human interference, and all events as well as men contribute to its progress."[9]

We may wish to grant Tocqueville a certain measure of hyperbole in this passage. We may also want to note that in his second volume several years later he was more troubled by what he viewed as some of the undesirable consequences of democracy and equality. Even so, he did not doubt that a continuing advance of democracy and equality was inevitable. If today we look back to the changes since his time, we, like Tocqueville in his own day, may well be amazed at the extent to which ideas and practices that respect and promote political equality have advanced across so much of the world—and, for that matter, aspects of a broader human equality as well.

As to political equality, consider the incredible spread of democratic ideas, institutions, and practices during the century just ended. In 1900, forty-eight countries were fully or moderately independent countries. Of these, only eight possessed all the other basic institutions of representative democracy, and in only one of these, New Zealand, had women gained the right to vote. Furthermore, these eight countries contained no more than 10 to 12 percent of the world's population. At the opening of our present century, among some one hundred ninety countries the political institutions and practices of modern representative democracy, including universal suffrage, exist in around eighty-five, at levels comparable to those in Britain, western Europe, and the United States. These countries include almost six out of every ten inhabitants of the globe today.[10]

In Britain, as we all know, the working classes and women were enfranchised, and more. Men and women of middle, lower middle, and working class origins not only gained access to the House of Commons and its facilities but to the cabinet and even the post of prime minister. And the hereditary peers in the House of Lords have, after all, at last been sent packing—well, most of them. In the United States, too, women were enfranchised; the Voting Rights Act of 1965 protecting the right of African Americans to vote did in fact become law; the law was actually enforced; and African Americans have become a significant force in American political life. I wish I could say that the miserable condition of so many Native Americans had greatly changed for the better, but that sad legacy of human injustice remains with us.

Failures and all, if we simply assume that beliefs about equality are always hopelessly anemic contestants in the struggle against the powerful forces that generate inequalities, we could not possibly account for the enormous gains for human equality over the past two centuries. Yet the question remains: given all the obstacles to political equality, how can we account for these gains?

A BRIEF SKETCH OF MOVEMENTS TOWARD POLITICAL EQUALITY

To help us understand how change toward political equality may come about despite the superior resources of the privileged strata, I want to present a schematic portrayal of the process.[11]

PRIVILEGE IS JUSTIFIED BY DOCTRINE

The most highly privileged members of a society—the political, social, and economic elites, if you will—typically espouse and, when they can, even enforce doctrines that justify their superiority. Often these doctrines are supported, and perhaps have been created, by religious authorities who themselves are members of the upper strata—as with "the divine right of kings" that over many centuries served in Europe to justify the rule of monarchs. Philosophers also contribute to the defense of elite rule—famously and enduringly in the case of Plato. But even the more moderate Aristotle was not particularly sympathetic with idea of political equality. In some cases, hierarchy and privilege may be legitimized by an official philosophy, as with Confucianism, which prevailed for several thousand years in imperial China. In recent totalitarian regimes, a dogmatic and unquestionable ideology has served to give legitimacy to power and privilege: Marxism-Leninism in the Soviet

Union, Fascist doctrine in Italy, the dogmas of Nazism in Hitler's Germany.

Privileged elites often appear to believe that their legitimizing doctrines are generally accepted among the lower strata: "Upstairs" assumes that its entitlements are accepted as perfectly legitimate by the inferior orders "Downstairs." Yet despite the fervent efforts of elites to promote views intended to give legitimacy to their superior power and status and their own unquestioning belief in the rightness of their entitlements, doubts arise among many members of subordinate groups that the inferior positions assigned to them by their self-proclaimed superiors are really justified.

James Scott has shown pretty convincingly that people who have been relegated to subordinate status by history, structure, and elite belief systems are much less likely to be taken in by the dominant ideology than members of the upper strata are prone to assume. As one example, he writes that "among the untouchables of India there is persuasive evidence that the Hindu doctrines that would legitimize caste domination are negated, reinterpreted, or ignored. Scheduled castes are much less likely than Brahmins to believe that the doctrine of karma explains their present condition; instead they attribute their status to their poverty and to an original, mythical act of injustice."[12]

MORE FAVORABLE CONDITIONS

Given the open or concealed rejection of the elite ideology by members of the subordinate groups, a change in conditions, whether in ideas, beliefs, structures, generations, or whatever, offers the subordinate groups new opportunities to express their grievances. For a variety of reasons, the British were unable to impose their political, economic, and social structures on the colonials who emigrated to America in the seventeenth and eighteenth centuries. Sheer distance across the Atlantic, the ready availability in the colonies of property in land, new opportunities in commerce and finance, the resulting growth of a large class of independent farmers, businessmen, and artisans, and other differences between colonial America and the mother country offered the colonials much greater opportunities to engage effectively in political life than they had enjoyed in Britain.

GROWING PRESSURES FOR CHANGE

With the emergence of these new opportunities, and driven by anger, resentment, a sense of injustice, a prospect of greater individual or group opportunities, group loyalty, or other motives, some members of the subordinate groups begin to press for change by any available means. For example, following the introduction of democracy in India, the members of the lower castes quickly began to seize their new opportunities to improve their status.

SUPPORT WITHIN THE DOMINANT STRATA

Some members of the dominant group choose to support the claims of the subordinate strata. Insiders ally themselves with outsiders—an Upstairs rebel takes on the cause of the discontented Downstairs. Insiders may do so for a variety of reasons: moral convictions, compassion, opportunism, fear of the consequences of disorder, dangers to property and the legitimacy of the regime, and even the real or imagined possibility of revolution.

THE SUBORDINATE STRATA MAKE GAINS

These factors culminate in a change by which the previously subordinate strata make significant gains in power, influence, status, education, income, or other advantages—and quite possibly all of these. For example, among the colonials in America the percentage of white males who gained the right to vote in elections to local and colonial legislatures was far higher than in the home country.[13] Sometimes, as was ultimately true in America, the gains are achieved, at least in part, by means of a violent revolution in which the subordinate strata overturn the dominance of the privileged strata. In many cases, however, change occurs more gradually and peacefully, as with the expansion of the suffrage by acts of parliament in Britain, Sweden, and other European countries, and by constitutional amendment and congressional action in the United States.

Although specific accounts of the changes toward political equality that have occurred in so many countries over the last several centuries would vary enormously, these general factors would, I believe, have played a part in most of them.

CHAPTER 3
...
Is Political Equality Achievable?

L et's assume that my sketch of political movements leading to greater political equality is roughly correct. It still leaves open a crucial question: what actually *drives* some persons in the privileged and subordinate strata to insist on greater political equality? Why do the subordinates Downstairs claim that they should be treated as *political* equals of the privileged Upstairs who rule over them? Are there aspects of "human nature" or human capacities that can be and sometimes have been evoked to drive people to make such demands? If we assume that political equality is an end or goal that is justifiable on basic ethical grounds, but definitely is not a description of actual conditions that must necessarily prevail among human beings, must we then assume that moves toward political equality are driven solely by ethical concerns? Or, as I've already suggested in my schematic scenario, may a search for political equality be driven also by "baser" motives? To repeat: what drives people to *act* in ways that will help to bring about changes that will actually enhance political equality?

Reason? Egoism? Altruism? Compassion? Empathy? Envy? Anger? Hatred? Any or all of these?

At this point, one might object that the question of why we *ought* to pursue political equality as an end is different (epistemologically and ontologically) from the question of why some persons actually *do* seek that end. I believe this to be a valid point. We owe to David Hume and Immanuel Kant, among others, the clear distinction between moral propositions asserting how human beings *ought to behave,* and empirical propositions asserting how human beings *actually* behave or tend to behave. To blur or overlook this distinction is to commit what has come to be called the "pathetic" fallacy.

Yet a moral obligation would become irrelevant to human action if it obliged us to perform actions and behavior so far removed from basic aspects of our human nature—in particular, our human drives, feelings, and emotions—as to render the obligation completely out of reach of human attainment. "Love thy neighbor" is highly demanding; but it draws on fundamental qualities of human beings—our capacities for love, compassion, empathy, sympathy—that sometimes enable us to obey it. "Love every human being just as much as you do a member of your own family" would demand action hopelessly beyond human reach. Unless the search for political equality is driven by some basic aspects of human beings, for all practical purposes it would be an irrelevant goal.

I raise these questions because some of our most distinguished philosophers have, I believe, placed too much weight on the strength of human reason as a force for justice or fairness. I want to suggest instead that what actually drives the search for fairness is not pure reason but emotions and passions. Reason may serve to guide action toward justice. It may (and I believe should) assist us in choosing the most efficient means to good ends. But what impels action are emotions like those I've already named, which range from compassion to envy, anger, and hatred.[1] David Hume forcefully made this point nearly three centuries ago, when he insisted that "reason is and ought to be only the slave of passions and can never pretend to any other office than to serve and obey them."[2] To Hume, deductive reasoning and empirical knowledge about causation were important instruments in choosing the best or most efficient means to our ends or goals. But in choosing the moral or ethical goals we actually pursue, we are driven, Hume argued, not by reason but by the power of our feelings and passions.

IS PURE REASON ENOUGH?

To some the observation that we are driven not by our reason but by our feelings, emotions, passions—call them what you will—may seem so self-evident that it needs no demonstration. Perhaps so. I would not press the question if it were not for influential views, as I just mentioned, that insist on the preponderant power of human reason to achieve good and just ends. Probably the most extreme argument of this kind was advanced by Immanuel Kant.

Having distinguished between "what is" and "what ought to be," Kant, one of the most distinguished philosophers of all time, held that reason not only can serve as a guide in our search for justice; it is the *only* part of human nature that can properly impel us toward moral action. In his *Groundwork of the Metaphysics of Morals* (1785) he wrote: "Every one must admit that a law has to carry with it absolute necessity if it is to be valid morally. . . . [C]onsequently the ground of obligation must be looked for, not in the nature of man nor in the circumstances of the world in which he is placed, but solely *a priori* in the concept of pure reason."

He offers an example: "To help others where when one can is a duty and besides this there are many spirits of so sympathetic a temper that, without any further motive of vanity or self-interest, they find an inner pleasure in spreading happiness around them and can take delight in the contentment of others as their own work. Yet I maintain that in such a case an action of this kind, however right and however amiable it may be, has still *no genuinely moral worth*.[3]"

In short, unless they were driven exclusively by "reason," all those who have helped to bring about greater political equality during recent centuries were not acting morally![4] Fortunately, something more is at work in human behavior than pure reason.

REASONING BEHIND A VEIL OF IGNORANCE

Probably no philosophic work stimulated more serious reflection on principles of justice in the twentieth century than John Rawls's highly original *A Theory of Justice* (1971).[5] Although no short summary could adequately set forth his argument, much less the enormous volume of comments, reflections, and criticism that it provoked,[6] I want to mention the assumptions about human nature on which his theory of justice is erected. Unlike Kant, Rawls's human beings are recognizable as our fellow creatures. "Let us assume," he writes, "that each person beyond a certain age and possessed of the requisite intellectual capacity develops a sense of justice under normal social circumstances. We acquire a skill in judging things to be just and unjust, and in supporting these judgments by reasons. Moreover, we ordinarily have some desire to act in accord with these pronouncements and expect a similar desire on the part of others. Clearly this moral capacity is extraordinarily complex. To see this it suffices to note the potentially infinite number and variety of judgments that we are prepared to make."[7]

He goes on to describe a hypothetical situation, "the original position": "The original position is not, of course, thought of as an actual historical state of affairs, much less as a primitive condition of culture. It is understood as a purely hypothetical situation. . . . Among the essential features of this situation is that no one knows his place in society, his class position or social status, nor does anyone know his fortune in the distribution of natural assets and abilities, his intelligence, strength, and the like. I shall even assume that the parties do not know their conceptions of the good or their special psychological propensities. The principles of justice are chosen behind a veil of ignorance."[8]

He then proposes "the two principles of justice that I believe would be chosen in the original position" behind the veil of ignorance. These are: "First: each person is to have an equal right to the most extensive liberty compatible with a similar liberty for others. Second: social and economic inequalities are to be arranged so that they are both (a) reasonably expected to be to everyone's advantage, and (b) attached to positions and offices open to all."

It should come as no surprise that a commitment to the first principle would, in Rawls's view, "secure the equal liberties of citizenship . . . since citizens of a just society are to have the same basic rights." In other words, the first principle would require political equality among citizens and all the institutions necessary to insure political equality. Although the second principle would allow for some inequalities, "[t]he distribution of wealth and income, and the hierarchies of authority, must be consistent with both the liberties of equal citizenship and equality of opportunity."[9]

Thus Rawls provides a powerful argument for political equality based on a much more realistic view of human beings than Kant's impossibly narrow vision. With Rawls, the goal of political equality is justified by reason, but reason is aided by a capacity for moral judgment derived from experience and, perhaps, basic aspects of human nature.

Like most philosophers in the twentieth century, Rawls was too aware of the fallacy of confusing "ought" with "is" to offer his argument as an empirical description of what actually drives people to search for political equality. Although he provides a powerful justification, one far better informed about human capacities than Kant's, we still need to confront our nagging question: What actually pushes people to struggle for greater political equality—sometimes, as in the struggle for civil and political rights for African Americans, against the seemingly overpowering forces of the status quo?

CHAPTER 4

A Respectable Role for Emotions

A s I have already suggested, the motivations that drive people to change the status quo in order to achieve greater political equality—fighting for civil rights and the extension of the suffrage, for example—appear to cover a wide range, from altruism, compassion, empathy, and sympathy to envy, anger, indignation, and hatred.

A HINT FROM CAPUCHIN MONKEYS

An interesting experiment with capuchin monkeys offers an intriguing hint. I say "hint" because I want to avoid the kind of simplistic and reductionist argument that leaps from animal behavior, or in even more extreme cases, from genes and chromosomes, to complex human behavior and institutions.[1] But the experiment does hint at the possibility that what drives individuals and groups to insist on distributive justice and fairness lies in emotions and feelings that can be traced far back in human evolution.

Female capuchin monkeys were taught to exchange

tokens—granite pebbles—with the experimenter in return for grapes and cucumbers. Previous experiments had shown that in 90 percent of the trials the female monkeys preferred grapes to cucumber slices, and that in less than 5 percent of the cases they failed to hand back the token in exchange for the food. Two monkeys were then placed in their cages in pairs so that each could see the other and observe which of the two rewards the other received. The experimenters observed that if one monkey was given a cucumber in return for her pebble but saw that the other received the more valued grape, the former often reacted by either refusing to hand over the pebble or choosing not to eat the cucumber.

The researchers concluded that: "People judge fairness based both on the distribution of gains and on the possible alternatives to a given outcome. Capuchin monkeys, too, seem to measure reward in relative terms, comparing their own reward with those available, and their own efforts with those of others. They respond negatively to previously acceptable rewards if a partner gets a better deal. Although our data cannot elucidate the precise motivations underlying these responses, one possibility is that monkeys, similarly to humans, are guided by social emotions. These emotions, known as 'passions' by economists, guide human reactions to the efforts, gains, losses and attitudes of others.[2]"

. . . TO HUMAN BEINGS

As I warned earlier, I don't assume that we can jump from an experimental result with capuchin monkeys to human behavior. Yet as a writer in the *New York Times* put it in his report on the experiment with capuchin monkeys: "'It's not fair!' is a common call from the playground and, in subtler form, from more adult assemblies. It now seems that monkeys, too, have a sense of fairness."[3] Many parents of two or more children have no doubt heard this same cry, often accompanied on the part of the sibling who utters it by rage, tears, or other spontaneous expressions of feeling.

My point, then, is simply that human beings are naturally endowed with a sensitivity to the unequal distribution of rewards to others whom they view as comparable to themselves in relevant ways. Whether like the authors of the study we describe this sensitivity by the aseptic term *inequity aversion,* or use earthier language like *jealousy* or *envy,* what a human being sees as unfairness or injustice will often arouse strong emotions. Given the opportunity, these emotions will then express themselves in actions, which may range from an immediate verbal expression—"It's not fair!"—to behavior intended to bring about a fairer distribution, whether by peaceful persuasion or violence, and whether by acting individually or in concert with others.

THE LIMITS OF REASON

It is true, certainly, that human beings are endowed with an extraordinary capacity for *reasoning*. But the way this capacity develops and is employed depends greatly on a person's own experience—on nurture, again, not nature.

For as the neurologist Antonio Damasio observes, reason simply *cannot* be separated from emotions and feelings, or from learning and experience. Feelings, he argues, are an inherent and inescapable part of the process of human reasoning and human deciding. From evidence about the behavior of persons whose prefrontal cortices have been damaged or destroyed, he concludes that although these persons may sometimes retain their "intelligence" as measured by IQ tests, they have lost their capacity for *judgment*. Their capacity for abstract "reason" is not impaired; indeed, their "reason" is completely detached from their emotions and feelings: perfect subjects for Kant's categorical imperative. But judgment, he concludes, depends on "knowledge" and experience that is stored up in the somatic system—in short, rooted in emotions and feelings derived from previous experiences.[4] Abstract reason is not a substitute for practical judgment; and a high cognitive intelligence—as measured by IQ—seems to be independent of "social intelligence" as well as other possible forms of intelligence or understanding, such as esthetic understanding.

Indeed, the way the brain itself develops is strongly dependent on experience. Nature, in the shape of genes, provides us with a brain. But the genes do not, in Damasio's words, "specify the entire structure of the brain . . . [M]any structural features are determined by genes, but another large number can be determined only by the activity of the living organism itself, as it develops and continuously changes throughout its life span."[5] In short, nature endows us with a brain. But experience—nurture—shapes it.

EMPATHY AND SYMPATHY

Human beings, like many other animals, are moved to act by more than purely self-interested egoism. Human beings are capable of identifying with others, so strongly that the hurt or well-being of another becomes hurt or well-being for oneself. Indeed, the capacity for identifying with others makes the very notion of "self" ambiguous. Does a mother think only of her own self and not of her beloved children, does a brother feel regard only for himself and not for his beloved siblings, do the children of aging or disabled parents have no feelings for their problems? To assume so would be to ignore basic aspects of human nature that—here a nod to the Darwinian paradigm—have been necessary for the survival of the species itself.

Although other primates—notably the anthropoid apes

like chimpanzees and bonobos—appear to experience empathy,[6] the capacity "to put oneself in another person's shoes" is particularly conspicuous among human beings. Here again, our genetic endowment, our inherent human nature, provides us with the capacity for empathy, or at least the potentiality for developing it.

Language, reason, intuition, and feelings like empathy help us to learn how to cooperate with others, to act in cooperation with others in order to build organizations and institutions, to work within their limits, and to alter them. Neither language, reason, intuition, empathy, nor feelings alone would be sufficient: they all seem to be necessary for human cooperation in organizations, complex processes, and institutions.

THE LIMITS OF EMPATHY

Yet empathy has distinct limits. It is impossible for us to experience love, affection, sympathy, and empathy for every human being with the same power that we feel for the precious few at the psychic center of our lives. If you harbor any doubts of the rapidly diminishing power of love and empathy, a test is readily at hand. I suggest that you compare the sacrifices you would be willing to make in order to prevent the death of a single member of your family or one of your closest friends with the sacrifices you would make to prevent the deaths of thousands in a flood or famine in some distant part of the world where you know not a single person. Or consider loss as you might measure it by the extent of your grief. It is humanly impossible for the strength of your grief over the loss of, say, one member of your family to be multiplied a thousandfold by those distant deaths of thousands of human beings whom you have never encountered. I say humanly impossible because if your grief were multiplied in that fashion, your life would become literally unbearable.

What a bit of honest introspection will confirm in each of us, I believe, is that empathy is a limited force for inducing us to sacrifice our own well-being or that of those who are closest to us—a rather small number of persons—for the benefit of distant others. Here I'll make another bow to neo-Darwinian conjectures: if the harm done to every other human being (let alone other creatures) whose suffering we learn about were to cause us as much pain and emotional discomfort as the suffering of those few persons to whom we are most deeply attached, it is hard to see how we would survive, not just as individuals but as a species. The limits on empathy, it appears, are necessary to life.

To return now to political equality: if unaided egoism is too weak a force for mobilizing us to act directly on behalf of the basic rights of distant others, so too is empathy. Yet in some times and places, combinations of egoism, empathy, sympathy, rationality, language, and communication help some groups of human beings to construct cultures and institutions, including political cultures and institutions, that operate to protect the basic rights of distant, unknown, and unknowable others, including the basic rights necessary to political equality.

AND THE PRIVILEGED STRATA?

Although it may seem obvious why members in the subordinate strata might be moved to action, why do members of the privileged strata often help to provide leadership from within their positions of authority? If not always from empathy or sympathy, then what? Earlier I mentioned that they may sometimes be driven by a fear of violence or even revolution, which might well prove far more costly than yielding at least some of their privileges to members of the deprived strata.

As Joseph Hamburger has shown, to bring about the expansion of the suffrage (and ultimately the passage of the Reform Act of 1832), James Mill, the father of John Stuart Mill and himself an eminent creator of the philosophy of utilitarianism, deliberately set out to create a fear of revolution among members of the British oligarchy. Although James Mill himself was opposed to violence as a means to bring about change, "Since Mill wished to achieve fundamental reforms without violence, it became necessary to devise means by which an oligarchy would be led to grant concessions out of self-interest. . . . [T]here were only two alternatives: '[The people] can only obtain any considerable amelioration in their government by resistance, by applying physical force to their rulers, or at least, by threats so likely to be followed by performance, as may frighten their rulers into compliance.' Since the use of physical force was to be avoided, Mill built his hopes on the second alternative . . . Mill was proposing that revolution be threatened. He assumed that the threat would be sufficient and that it would not be necessary to carry it out."[7] The Reform Act of 1832, which Mill helped thereby to bring about, was the first of a series of suffrage reforms that would finally culminate with universal adult suffrage.

In the United States, the threat of revolution played no significant part in securing the passage of legislation that helped Southern blacks to gain entry at last into American political life: the Civil Rights Acts of 1957 and 1964 and the Voting Rights Act of 1965. The Civil Rights Act of 1957 reversed a century of votes by Southern U.S. senators who had steadily defeated legislation intended to protect the voting rights of African Americans. Though weakened by compromises to gain the necessary votes in the Senate, the bill helped Southern blacks to gain entry at last into American political life, completing much of what had begun a decade earlier. The historic change in 1957 (weak as it was) could not have been achieved without the energy and skills of the Senate leader, Lyndon Johnson[8]—who employed them again as president to secure the passage of the more robust laws of 1964 and 1965. The emotions that supported his relentless effort to gain their passage were complex. His private feelings about African Americans were mixed, combining elements of empathy with residues of prevailing Southern prejudice derived from his Texan background. But the driving force behind his efforts was his incessant political ambition. No one who knew Johnson would have described him as a man for whom sympathy alone would have driven him to invest the enormous time, energy, and skill that he devoted to bringing about the passage of these laws, whether as majority leader or president. Throughout much of his life Johnson was driven by political ambition, which even before the 1950s had become focused on the supreme prize, the presidency of the United States. It is hardly open to doubt that Johnson's ambition to become president drove his actions on civil rights as Senate Majority Leader, and, as president, no doubt his ambition for re-election was a powerful impetus for employing his skills and influence to win the passage of the Civil Rights Act of 1964. It seems likely that in 1965 he was spurred, in some part, by his desire to complete what he had begun and thus to ensure his "place in history."[9]

GAINS FOR POLITICAL EQUALITY

So a seismic shift occurs. Following the extension of the franchise and effective legal protection of basic rights, leaders of hitherto subordinate groups enter into public competition and some are elected to public office. Changes in law and policy follow.

As with the foothold in the House of Commons gained by the middle classes in Britain after 1832, so, too, in the United States after 1965: African Americans seized their opportunities to vote—and among other actions soon tossed out the elected police officials who had violently enforced their earlier subordination. So, too, in India: after the lower castes gained the franchise in a country with acceptably free and fair elections, they began to vote in substantial numbers for leaders who were committed to reducing discrimination against them. Thus "by the early Nineties pan-Indian upper-caste dominated parties . . . could gain power in New Delhi only with the help of small regional powers that, more often than not, represented newly empowered lower-cast Hindus."[10]

FROM INITIAL VICTORIES TO POLITICAL INSTITUTIONS

One of the aspects of our human nature that distinguishes us from all other living beings is an extraordinary capacity for cooperation that enables us to create organizations of a complexity that is unmatched in any other species.[11] To be sure, without genes that enable some degree of cooperation, few if any other species—monkeys, elephants, wolves, ants, bees, or other creatures—would have survived, much less evolved. However, thanks to the genetic evolution of human beings over some millions of years, we can and do construct systems of cooperation that in their extent and complexity are unique among all living beings.

Human beings not only create complex organizations and processes. We also make them into highly durable *institutions,* practices so firmly embedded in habits, behaviors, and beliefs that they are passed on from one generation to the other, often with only minor modifications. Obviously, gains for political equality would prove ephemeral unless they were anchored in enduring institutions—legal and administrative systems, for example, that will enforce newly enacted laws intended to protect the voting rights of newly enfranchised groups.

I shall not attempt here to describe the processes by which elements of a human system become institutionalized and thus endure even after the original innovators have achieved their initial goals. I want only to emphasize that, whatever the emotional drives that helped to bring about a change toward political equality, to sustain that achievement requires means that will probably draw on somewhat different emotional and cognitive resources. With their extraordinary achievements in the 1950s and 1960s, civil rights movements in the United States may have lost much of their zeal, but their gains were preserved by enduring legal and bureaucratic institutions staffed by persons who draw on skills and emotions that may differ from those of their founders.

CONCLUSION

Yes, political equality is (in my view) an ideal we should strive to attain, a moral obligation to act in its support. And yes, too, the obstacles to attaining political equality are great—so great, indeed, that we shall almost certainly remain forever some considerable distance from fully achieving that goal.

Yet efforts to achieve the goal in the face of often formidable efforts by privileged strata to preserve their positions are driven by very powerful human emotions that can be mobilized and, with the aid of reason in selecting the appropriate means, can bring about gains for political equality.

Over the past two centuries, through much of our world these gains have exceeded any before achieved in all human history.

Can further gains be made in democratic countries? Or have we reached our limits? Or, worse, is the coming century likely to see a regressive shift toward greater political *in*equality?

CHAPTER 5

Political Equality, Human Nature, and Society

The obstacles to political equality have always and everywhere been formidable. Indeed, they are so daunting that even when the basic human drives we explored in the last chapter are mobilized under relatively favorable historical conditions, the extent to which the goal is actually achieved is bound to be rather limited. A gain that is enormous from a historical perspective may seem modest when measured against ideal standards.

In this chapter I want to describe some fundamental obstacles that have held us below a threshold that we have not yet been able to cross even in democratic countries. The barriers to political equality that I want to describe briefly are:

1. The distribution of political resources, skills, and incentives.
2. Irreducible limits on time.
3. The size of political systems.

4. The prevalence of market economies.

5. The existence of international systems that may be important but are not democratic.

6. The inevitability of severe crises.

1. POLITICAL RESOURCES, SKILLS, AND INCENTIVES

Running directly counter to political equality is a fundamental law governing human nature and human society:

Political resources, knowledge, skills, and incentives are always and everywhere distributed unequally.

A *political resource* is any means that a person can use to influence the behavior of other persons. Political resources therefore include money, information, time, understanding, food, the threat of force, jobs, friendship, social standing, effective rights, votes, and a great many other things. Of these, quite possibly the only ones that are distributed equally are, in democratic systems, the fundamental rights necessary to democracy that I described in the last chapter. Among these perhaps the most obvious is the right to vote. In order for (adult) citizens to be considered political equals, the vote of each must be counted as equal to the votes of others. So, too, in legislatures: if elected representatives are to be equal, they must have equal votes.

In order for citizens to exercise their right to vote effectively, democratic political systems must impose *duties* on officials and on all other citizens to respect and enforce the right to an equal vote, and to ensure that all citizens have an adequate *opportunity* to vote.

Yet even if adequate rights, duties, and opportunities guarantee equal votes, the other political resources I have named are distributed unequally in all democratic systems. Might not the unequal distribution of political resources produce inequalities in the capacity of different citizens to employ their votes effectively to protect and advance their interests, goals, and ends?

Not only are political resources distributed unequally. So, too, are the capacities of citizens to use their political resources efficiently and effectively to achieve their goals—i.e., their *political knowledge* and *skills.*

KNOWLEDGE

The complexity of public policies often makes it difficult, sometimes perhaps even impossible, for ordinary citizens to understand them sufficiently well to know where their interests lie. Does a particular policy on the public agenda protect or advance their interests? Harm them? Do some of both but, on balance, come out more favorable than harmful—or the reverse?

The problem exists whether one defines a citizen's interest narrowly or broadly. From a classical perspective, does the policy serve the public interest or the general good—however one might choose to define these difficult concepts? From a common modern perspective, does the policy benefit or harm the basic interests of this particular citizen or others whose interests the citizen most deeply cares about?

An accumulation of many decades of evidence from systematic surveys of public attitudes and opinions since their inception in the 1940s seems to indicate that in all democratic countries the average citizen falls pretty far short of the good citizen as portrayed either in the classical or modern formulation. Citizens who are deeply interested in politics constitute a minority. Except for voting, even fewer actively engage in politics, whether by attempting to persuade others to vote for a candidate, working for a political party, attending political meetings and rallies, or joining political organizations. And in spite of a flood of easily accessible news and information, the average citizen's knowledge of political issues and candidates is meager.

SKILLS

An ordinary Athenian could not match the skill of Pericles as an orator and thus his capacity to influence other citizens in voting in the assembly. Nor could a British citizen match the oratorical skills of Winston Churchill, nor an American those of FDR. And political skills include far more than oratory: although Lyndon Johnson was no great orator, he possessed exceptional skill in using all the resources he had at his disposal—as he demonstrated, for example, when he managed to secure the epochal change represented by the passage and enforcement of the Civil Rights Acts.[1] Persons with superior political skills not only can employ them to attain "the public good"; they can also use them to achieve their own personal ends, possibly at the expense of other citizens.

INCENTIVES

Important as skills are, to gain political influence one must also possess an incentive to employ those skills in order to gain and exercise influence over political decisions. Of two persons with similar skills, one may be driven toward political life, another in a quite different direction. Lyndon Johnson might well have been a successful lawyer; but since childhood his ambition, it seems, was to succeed in politics and ultimately to become president. FDR might have lived out his life as a country gentleman, and Winston Churchill as a familiar member of the British aristocratic social scene.

Many persons who possess the appropriate resources, skills, and incentives to gain influence over political decisions may nonetheless choose not to seek elective public office. Instead, they may gain influence over government as civil servants or administrators, or by lobbying, providing funds, corrupting public officials, influencing public opinion, and a host of other ways. Indeed, many well-known theorists have contended that even in democratic countries (or pseudo-democracies, as these theorists might wish to call them) political life is always dominated by elites—particularly economic elites—whose influence may not necessarily be overt and may indeed be quite hidden.[2]

I have no wish to propose here a general theory about how political influence is distributed in democratic countries. My point is far simpler and, I believe, fairly obvious—though no less important because it is all but self-evident. Let me restate it: *Political resources, skills, and incentives are always and everywhere distributed unequally.*

2. LIMITS ON TIME

Throughout human history, in all societies most people have devoted a significant amount of their time attempting to influence the decisions of others in associations they believe are important to their lives: their family, tribe, workplace, neighborhood, business firm, professional association, trade union, club, church, or whatnot. In that sense, the use of influence, power, and authority is spread throughout all of human life, and "politics" is universal.

But it is quite something else for people to devote much of

their time in attempting to influence the government of the *state*. To be sure, throughout much of human history most persons were provided with few if any opportunities to influence the government of the state to which they were subject. But with the arrival and spread of popular governments— "democracies"—and the broadening of citizenship and the suffrage in the nineteenth and twentieth centuries, half or more of adult humankind came to possess all the rights and opportunities they needed in order to engage peacefully in attempting to influence the decisions of government of the state whose laws and policies they were obligated to obey. Yet it is an easily observable fact that while a small minority of persons in democratic countries spend a large portion of their time seeking and employing political influence, the great majority of citizens do not.

Because time is a scarce and fixed resource, using one's time on one activity necessarily reduces the amount of time one can spend on other activities. This elementary fact of life has some inescapable consequences for political equality.

1. Actions undertaken to gain political influence require time. Different persons make different assessments of the costs and benefits of using their time to gain political influence. Those who are willing to spend more time are more likely to gain greater influence over political decisions. Thus, holding all else the same, unequal time spent

by different citizens leads to unequal influence, which, in turn, leads to political inequality among citizens.

2. Even in political units small enough to allow citizens to participate directly in making political decisions, differences in the perceived costs and benefits of using time will result in some political inequality among citizens. At the height of Athenian democracy in the fifth-century B.C., "in practice not more than a fraction of the citizen population were ever present."[3] As the number of citizens increases, the total amount of time required for each to participate *directly* in making governmental decisions soon reaches a point at which, even if they attend meetings, most citizens can no longer participate fully. Consider a citizen's right to speak at a town meeting. As the number of citizens who wish to exercise their right to speak increases, the costs in time rise steeply. In a unit with just twenty citizens, if each citizen were allowed to speak for ten minutes, the meeting would require two hundred minutes, or more than three hours. In a unit with fifty citizens, to allow each citizen to speak for ten minutes would require a full eight hour day; in a unit with five hundred citizens, more than ten eight hour days! As the number of citizens in a democratic political unit increases, the costs in time for direct participation rapidly reach impossible heights.

When the size of a unit grows too large for all citizens to participate directly in making laws, they face three alternatives. A democratic political unit larger than, say, twenty citizens may split up and form smaller units—hardly a practical solution in most cases. A second possibility is to restrict, with the formal or implicit consent of the citizens, the number of persons who might participate by speaking at the citizens' assembly. This solution may enable a unit such as a town to maintain a comparatively high level of political equality and democratic decision-making among its citizens.[4] But if the unit continues to grow in numbers (not to mention in the size of its territory) and the proportion of citizens who can actually participate directly grows smaller and smaller, even this arrangement will become impractical. An obvious way to deal with the problem of size is now to allow citizens to elect a small number of representatives who will devote more of their time to making decisions on behalf of all the members of the unit. This third solution has been adopted, of course, in all democratic countries. In effect, citizens *delegate* to representatives their authority to make decisions.

Thus we encounter another limit on the possibilities of political equality.[5]

The law of time and numbers: The more citizens a democratic unit contains, the less that citizens can participate directly in government decisions and the more that they must delegate authority to others.

3. THE DILEMMA OF SIZE

When we think about the "size" of a political unit, we might have several different dimensions in mind: for example, its total population, the number of its adult citizens, or the amount of territory occupied by the unit. For any particular political system these tend to be correlated. If the area that a political system controls grows larger, the number of persons included in the system will probably (though not necessarily) increase, and perhaps the number of adult citizens. In what follows I want to ignore territorial size and total population and focus solely on the number of adult citizens (whom I'll refer to simply as "citizens").

The law of time and numbers has a corollary:

The dilemma of size: The smaller a democratic unit, the greater its potential for citizen participation and the less the need for citizens to delegate government decisions to representatives. The larger the unit, the greater its capacity for dealing with problems important to its citizens and the greater the need for citizens to delegate decisions to representatives.

Before turning to the potentially adverse effects on political equality of increasing size, I want to mention a very important exception: If the increase in the number of citizens results from an increase in the proportion of the adult population who possess the full rights of citizenship—for example, by extending the franchise—then the favorable effects on political equality may more than offset any adverse effects resulting from increasing the number of citizens (as we'll see below). In what follows I'll ignore this possibility in order to maintain our focus on adult citizens.

Except in units of miniscule size, citizens must delegate considerable authority to others—persons who function as executives, administrators, agenda setters, judges, and others. In classical Athens, for example, citizens delegated the authority to set the agenda for the meetings of the assembly to a Council of Five Hundred (Boule), whose members were selected by lot. In New England town meetings, significant authority is delegated to an executive body—known in Connecticut, for example, as a Board of Selectmen, in which the First Selectman is, in effect, the mayor of the town. In larger systems like a metropolis, province, region, U.S. state, country, or international organization, authority to make administrative and judicial decisions is even more fully delegated.

Because delegates have greater opportunities to exercise direct influence over decisions than ordinary citizens, their authority poses problems for political equality. How can voters be sure that their elected and appointed delegates will strictly pursue policies that accurately represent their views or interests, or at any rate those of a majority of citizens? In short, how can citizens hold their delegates fully accountable?

Even when authority is delegated to elected representatives, size continues to exercise an influence. As the size of a unit increases, the number and complexity of public policies also are likely to increase, and demands on citizens' knowledge increasingly surpass the limits of their knowledge. For a citizen to gain a fair grasp of the issues in a town of five hundred or five thousand inhabitants is one thing; but it is quite another for that citizen to gain an adequate understanding of the political issues confronting a unit of a hundred thousand citizens, or one million, or one hundred million.

The size of a political unit also imposes practical limits on the number of persons serving in a representative body. And number of representatives interacts with time: the greater the number of citizens for each representative, the less time a representative will have available for meeting directly with a citizen or indirectly through mail, telephone, or electronic means like e-mail. Representatives may, and in modern representative bodies virtually all do, also appoint staff members to facilitate communication with constituents. Even so, time and numbers impose powerful limits on effective interchange.

Table 5.1. Legislative representation per population in
selected democratic countries.

Country	Total Number Elected to Legislature	Total Number Elected to Representative Chamber	Population (Millions)	Population per Each Member of Representative Chamber
Australia	226	150	19.9	132,754
Austria	245	183	8.2	44,671
Belgium	221	150	10.3	68,989
Canada	413	308	32.5	105,545
France	923	577	60.4	104,721
Germany	672	603	82.4	136,691
India	793	545	1,065.0	1,954,258
Italy	945	630	58.1	921,55
Japan	722	480	127.3	265,277
Mexico	628	500	105.0	209,919
Spain	609	259	40.2	155,524
United Kingdom	1259	659	60.3	91,458
United States	535	435	293.0	673,627
Average	630	421	151.0	310,430

Source: The CIA World Factbook, http://www.cia.gov/cia/publications/factbook/

Although legislatures in modern democratic countries
vary considerably in size, in all of them the number of persons theoretically represented by a member is enormous
(Table 5.1).

Americans elect one member of Congress for about every

673,000 persons; Germans, one for about every 137,000. In the extreme case, India, the proportion is one member for nearly every two million persons. Even the smaller democratic countries cannot escape the limits of size. As a consequence, even with the most up-to-date technology a member of parliament in a democratic country could engage in a serious and extended discussion with only a microscopic percentage of the member's constituents.

My point here is not that increasing the size of a political system and delegating authority are undesirable. On the contrary, on balance they may well be highly desirable. But in coping with the dilemma of size by increasing the number of persons included in the political system, we inevitably create obstacles to achieving political equality among all citizens.

4. THE PRESENCE OF A MARKET ECONOMY

An important force for increasing the size of political systems is the presence of a market economy as a major institution for the distribution of goods and services.

Through the nineteenth and much of the twentieth centuries, many intellectuals, politicians, workers, and others supported alternatives in which economic firms would be converted to entities owned and operated by the state or perhaps changed into cooperatives owned and operated by workers or consumers. In many of these socialist visions, decisions that were determined in capitalist systems mainly by markets—prices, wages, and outputs, for example—would be made wholly or in part by government officials or by some other alternative to markets.[6] I have, of course, drastically simplified the programmatic proposals of socialists and other critics of capitalism. My point is, however, that well before the end of the twentieth century these alternatives to market capitalism had virtually disappeared from the public agenda. They lingered on only as historical residues in the names of center-left political parties—socialist, social democratic—that had abandoned their earlier dreams of a socialist or communist society, and no major party in any advanced democratic country actually advocated moving toward the socialist goal of "social ownership of the means of production."

Contrary to the views of socialists, advocates of central planning, and other critics who hoped to replace markets wholly or mainly with a nonmarket economy of some kind, twentieth century experience demonstrated pretty conclusively that a nonmarket economy is both highly inefficient and, because of the power to control economic decisions that it necessarily places in the hands of governments, incompatible with democratic controls over leaders. A modern market economy, on the other hand, where countless decisions are made by innumerable actors, each relatively independent of the others, acting from rather narrow self-regarding interests, and guided by information supplied by markets, produces goods and services much more efficiently than any known alternative, with a regularity and orderliness that is truly astonishing.[7]

What is more, the decentralization of decisions to numerous firms helps to prevent the high degree of centralization of power characteristic of centrally directed economies. This feature and others help to render a market economy more compatible with democracy than the centralized, state-run economies that were so prominent a feature of many authoritarian and totalitarian countries.

Yet with all its advantages a market economy has two adverse consequences that create persistent problems in a democratic order.

First, without regulation—and even with it—a market economy inevitably and almost constantly inflicts harm on some people, and at times on many. The manifold harms caused by the dynamic changes that constantly occur in a market economy are many. Among these are:

Unemployment
Employment only at jobs with lesser skills
Impoverishment

Persistent poverty

Inadequate shelter, extending from loss of family housing to
surviving on the street

Illness, physical impairment, and death resulting from conditions in the workplace

Damages to self-esteem, self-confidence, and respect

Loss of neighborhood and friends because of movement in
search of work.

*Second, a market economy—a capitalist market economy, at
any rate—inevitably generates a vast inequality in resources
among its citizens.* These inequalities extend not merely to
incomes and wealth but, directly and indirectly, to information, status, education, access to political elites, and many
others. As I have pointed out, resources like these are all
readily convertible to *political* resources, resources that can
be used to gain influence, authority, and power over others.
All the other sources of unequal political resources are enormously compounded by the inequalities in resources flowing
from a market economy.

Because democratic political institutions enable those who
are injured by markets to mobilize and seek changes, frequently with some success, the boundaries between free markets and government regulation are constantly in flux. Moreover, measures that were first enacted in Germany under the

leadership of Bismarck—hardly an advocate of socialism—and widely adopted during the twentieth century in all the advanced democracies (belatedly, even in the United States), considerably reduced the cruelty and harshness inherent in unregulated market capitalism. Ironically, by softening the harsh effects of a capitalist market economy on those who had been most vulnerable, the welfare state further reduced support for a nonmarket socialist economy.

To sum up: A market economy inevitably and frequently inflicts serious harm on some citizens. By producing great inequalities in resources among citizens, market capitalism inevitably also fosters political inequality among the citizens of a democratic country.

Yet a modern democratic country has no feasible alternative to an economy of market capitalism.

5. THE NEED FOR NONDEMOCRATIC INTERNATIONAL SYSTEMS

The problem that international systems pose for political equality can be summarized in the form of three simple propositions.[8]

- International systems make decisions that bear important consequences for, among others, citizens in democratic countries.

- Many of the decisions resulting from international systems lead to highly desirable results.
- Yet the decisions of international systems are not and probably cannot be made democratically.

The first proposition is scarcely open to question. To list only a few examples, consider the European Union, International Monetary Fund (IMF), World Bank, International Labor Organization, North American Free Trade Agreement, North Atlantic Treaty Organization, Organization of American States, United Nations, United Nations Development Program, World Health Organization . . .

Add to these the important consequences of global firms and markets.

Nor will many people question the second proposition, even though they may vigorously disagree about the desirability of specific decisions, consequences, organizations, and systems.

If the third proposition is correct, however, then we confront a deep and serious challenge to democracy and thereby to political equality

In speaking of *decisions* of international systems, I have in mind four basic sociopolitical processes for arriving at collective decisions: hierarchy, or control *by* leaders; bargaining, or control *among* leaders; the price system, or control *of* and *by* leaders; and democracy, or control *of* leaders.[9]

These are, of course, highly simplified and highly abstract types. In a modern democratic country none exists in pure form or in isolation from the others. Indeed, the closer we move toward observing and describing concrete systems the more complex the interconnections among the four theoretically distinguishable processes become. Nonetheless, my basic point can be fairly stated, I believe, as follows: International systems of decision-making include hierarchies, bargaining among elites, and the price system. What is conspicuously absent, or weak to the point of utter irrelevance, is effective *democratic* control over decision-makers.

Our question, then, becomes something like this: Can we expect international systems to develop the basic political institutions of modern representative democracy at a level equivalent to that in, for example, a democratic country? Several reasons justify a skeptical answer.

- To begin with, the institutions will have to be *deliberately created.* They will not come about through some form of spontaneous generation or blind Darwinian evolution. Yet with the possible exception of the European Union, I see virtually no prospect that a full set of genuine democratic institutions will be introduced in any international organization. It approaches utter absurdity, for example, to imagine that the decisions of the World Bank or the World Trade Organization (WTO) will one day be made by a legislative body composed of representatives directly elected by the people of the countries that are bound by their decisions

- Second, international systems greatly intensify the problems of size. If large countries already push the challenges to political equality to their limits, international systems push them even further.

- Third, diversity in historical experiences, identities, cultures, values, beliefs, loyalties, languages, and more makes the creation and operation of democratic institutions in international organizations even more unlikely. The relation between size and diversity is empirically and theoretically imperfect—consider the cultural diversities of Belgium or Switzerland, for example. But in general the relation is positive, in the sense that increasing size—not only in numbers of citizens but in area—tends to increase diversity. This outcome seems to me obviously true with international systems. For to the already existing diversities within countries, international systems add diversities within some countries that are by no means duplicated in others.

Because of diversity, decisions have different consequences for different groups. The costs and benefits of virtually all political decisions bear differently on different groups. There are always losers as well as gainers. Losers may yield unwillingly—or not at all. Even in democratic countries, losers or potential losers may resort to violence. In the United States in 1861, the result was civil war.

- Diversity suggests a fourth reason for skepticism: the need to create a political culture that will help to induce citizens to support their political institutions through times of conflict and crisis. Maintaining stability in time of acute crisis is difficult enough within democratic countries, particularly those with great diversity. (I'll return to the problem in a moment.) A generally democratic and constitutionally supportive political culture that Americans had developed over more than half a century proved too weak to prevent secession and civil war in 1861. But if crisis and conflict threaten cohesion even within a country with a widely shared political culture, language, and national identity, crisis and conflict will threaten cohesion even more in international systems that lack a widely shared political culture.

- Fifth, the complexity of many international decisions makes it extremely difficult and even impossible for most citizens to provide their *informed* consent to such decisions. Within democratic countries, citizens tend to be least well informed about foreign affairs. How could international systems succeed where national systems often fail?

• Finally, *the global economy, international markets, and international business firms* constitute an international system that poses peculiar and highly complex problems of legitimacy. Business firms that are predominantly hierarchical in their internal governments, but operate in more or less competitive markets, gain a substantial part of their public acceptability, toleration, and legitimacy not only from the benefits of market competition to consumers but also because of regulatory actions taken by the state. If the economic history of the past two centuries tells us anything, it is that state regulation is absolutely essential to insure a reasonable level of market competition, to reduce the harm otherwise caused by unregulated firms and markets, and to insure a more just, or at least more acceptable, distribution of the benefits. Without state regulation, political elites and the public at large would soon sweep private business firms and markets into that well-known dustbin of history.

How are business firms and markets to be regulated at the international level? One answer is that they will be regulated by other international organizations and processes—the WTO, World Bank, IMF, and the like. But doesn't that solution, desirable as it may be, simply restate our central problem of democratic consent in another way?

I do not mean to suggest that nondemocratic international systems are dictatorships. Perhaps our vocabulary lacks a satisfactory name for them. I would be inclined to call them *governments by limited pluralistic elites.* That is to say, in making their decisions, *international political and bureaucratic elites* are *limited* by treaties, international agreements, and the ultimate threat of national rejection; and they are typically *pluralistic* because of the diversity of views, loyalties, and obligations among the elites.

6. CRISES

It seems to me reasonably safe to offer another fundamental law of politics: *From time to time every political system is likely to face serious crises.*

These include acute internal conflict, civil war, foreign aggression, international warfare, natural disasters, famine, economic depression, unemployment, acute inflation, and others. To this list we must now add the ever-present possibility of terrorist attacks.

In a country where democratic institutions are not firmly established and a democratic political culture is weak, a crisis may bring about a collapse and regression to dictatorship, as it frequently did in Latin American countries and elsewhere during the last century. But even in a country where democratic institutions and a supportive political culture are long-standing and relatively sturdy, a severe crisis is likely to bring about a shift of power away from elected representatives to the executive—from the Parliament or Congress to the prime minister or president.

The shift of power to the executive is likely to be particularly acute during times of crisis that involve areas of policy over which democratic controls, even in less stressful times, are weak—notably foreign and military affairs. For example, in the United States the control of the president over foreign policy has always been much stronger than that of the Congress. The increase in executive power and the diminution in legislative controls—not to say the influence of ordinary citizens—is particularly evident in the face of a threat of war, and even greater in the event of war itself. More recently, the threat of terrorism has emerged as a major factor in shifting power to the executive—notably from American citizens and the U.S. Congress to the president following the attacks of September 11, 2001. (I'll return to this experience in the next chapter.)

In drastically reducing political equality among citizens, the effects of international crises and the threat of terrorism are by no means unique to the United States. Perhaps no more dramatic evidence can be found for the extent to which crisis—foreign crisis—shifts power away from elected representatives and the public to the executive than that provided by Britain. There, the British prime minister and cabinet chose to support the United States in the invasion of Iraq despite the overwhelming, continuing, and even increasing opposition of the British public.

Fortunately, on many matters other than foreign affairs and war the levels of political equality among all citizens, including leaders, remained at or above the threshold existing in other countries we regard—whatever their shortcomings—as "democracies."

To sum up:

Always and everywhere, the goal of political equality among the citizens of a political unit faces formidable obstacles: the distribution of political resources, skills, and incentives; irreducible limits on time; the size of political systems; the prevalence of market economies; the existence of international systems that may be important but are not democratic; and the inevitability of severe crises.

Is it possible that in countries we now judge to be fully "democratic" we may push beyond these limits? Or, instead, might they prevent future progress toward that goal? Or, worse, might they cause reversals that will move democratic countries toward greater political inequality among their citizens? Might increasing political inequality push some countries—including the United States—below the threshold at which we regard them as "democratic," even though they may remain well above the level at which we can reasonably designate a country as "authoritarian," or a dictatorship, or the like?

In short, might the extraordinary historical era in which so many countries made the transition to "democracy" come to an end during our present century, and a new age emerge in which some well-established democratic countries sink into significantly less democratic forms of rule?

CHAPTER 6

Will Political Inequality Increase in the United States?

The future of political equality in democratic countries seems fraught with uncertainty.

Consider some possibilities. Perhaps the already existing levels of political equality and inequality will remain pretty much unchanged. Perhaps political inequalities will be reduced further and political equality will increase to a level closer to the ideal. Or perhaps the goal of political equality will become even more distant as the barriers to it continue to grow more difficult to overcome. A complex but not unrealistic possibility is that movement will occur in both directions: some barriers will be lowered while some will be raised, and the overall effect will be to keep the threshold about where it has been, with no significant net gain or loss for political equality. Or yet another possibility: the overall effect of changes up and down is a substantial decline in political equality, and citizens will be even more unequal in their influence on government decisions.

To make this array of uncertainties more manageable, I am going to restrict my discussion to the United States, and among the many possibilities I'll consider only two. In one, political inequality will increase substantially among American citizens. In the other, Americans will move closer to that elusive goal. I do not mean to imply that these two scenarios are much more likely than the others. However, each in its own way presents us with a special challenge.

A troublesome question now arises: In order to conclude that political inequality has increased or decreased, we need ways to *measure* the differences in distances from that elusive goal. I'll take up this problem next. (Some readers may wish to skip this discussion and move directly to my description of the two possible futures that I just mentioned.)

MEASURING POLITICAL INEQUALITY

Achieving truly well-grounded judgments about the future of political equality in the United States probably exceeds our capacities.

One reason is that, unlike wealth and income, or even health, longevity, and many other possible ends, to estimate gains and losses in political equality we lack cardinal measures that would allow us to say, for example, that "political equality is twice as great in country X as in country Y." At best we must rely on ordinal measures based on judgments about "more," "less," "about the same," and the like. We can conclude that from 1990 to 1999 GNP per capita in the

United States increased from $23,560 to $31,910, or 65 percent, and was about 25 percent larger than that of Germany and about 122 times than that of Nigeria. But we cannot assert that in the twenty years following the passage of the civil rights acts in the 1950s and 1960s, political equality increased in the United States by 15 percent (or whatever).

We might be able to develop *ordinal* measures, however, that would allow us to say that a given quality or institution is present to a greater or lesser extent: to say, for example, that "democracy" or "political equality" increased in the United States following the passage of the legislation I mentioned earlier that helped to protect the rights of African Americans to vote and participate actively in other political activities. We might even be able to conclude that political equality is at a *higher level* in country *X* than in country *Y*. Sometimes we can also arrive at solid qualitative judgments that are themselves *based on* quantitative indicators, as with changes that occurred when groups previously excluded, such as workers, women, and African Americans, gained the franchise and other important political rights.

More often, however, we must rely on *judgments by qualified observers* about the extent to which certain basic democratic institutions are present in a particular country. For some years, political scientists and others have drawn on judgments of this kind to rank different countries on a scale ranging from the most democratic to the least democratic. Table 6.1 provides a summary of rankings of 126 countries from most to least democratic. The rankings are based on judgments about the existence in 2000 of four of the political institutions essential for representative democracy that I described in Chapter 2:[1]

- Free, fair, and frequent elections.
- Freedom of expression.
- Alternative sources of information: free access by citizens to views other than those of officials.
- Associational autonomy: full freedom for political organizations, such as political parties, to form and engage in political activity.[2]

Given the importance of democratic political institutions for achieving political equality, for all its shortcomings an ordinal ranking like that shown in Table 6.1 can serve as a rough proxy for measuring political equality and inequality.

These and other similar classifications suffer, however, from two related deficiencies that are critical for this discussion. The upper and lower thresholds are somewhat arbitrary; and no distinctions are made among the "most democratic" countries or, at the other end, among the "least democratic." Thus the scales don't allow for the possibility that Norway, Sweden, or Switzerland might be somewhat

Table 6.1: Summary of Country Polyarchy Rankings: 1985 and 2000
(Number of Countries Ranked on Degree of Democracy)

Rank	1985	2000
1	10	26
2	8	15
3	1	25
4	13	16
5	10	13
6	9	9
7	19	2
8	19	7
9	7	4
10	27	9
Total	123	126

"more democratic" than France, Italy, or the United States
(and that important differences might also exist among the
least democratic, or most authoritarian, countries). Figure
6.1 compares 1985 and 2000 democratic accountability ratings of the thirty countries that make up the Organization
for Economic Cooperation and Development (OECD).

We now face a further troublesome deficiency: we have
no generally accepted names for political systems that fall
between the two ends of the scale. Although these political systems are not at the level of the "most democratic"

Figure 6.1. Summary of democratic accountability ratings of the thirty OECD countries: 1985 and 2000 (six-point scale, ranking from least to most democratic).

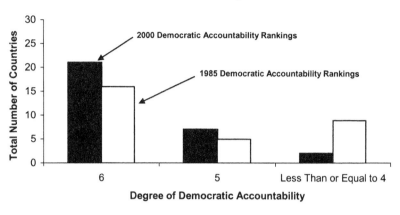

countries, they are above, perhaps well above, the level of the "least democratic" countries. Suppose that a decline in civil liberties caused by the threat of terrorism brings about changes in the United States that require it to be moved down from the "most democratic" category to a place lower on the scale, yet a level very far from the bottom—let us say, to scale type 4. To call such a country fascist, authoritarian, totalitarian, or a dictatorship, like those at scale type 10 or below, would be profoundly misleading—as any survivor of Fascist Italy under the dictatorship of Benito Mussolini, Nazi Germany under Hitler, the USSR under Stalin, or Argentina, Chile, and Uruguay under their military regime would be the first to insist. Whatever we choose to call it, the United States will no longer be among the countries at the top of an acceptable scale that run from most to least democratic. That is to say, it will no longer be a democracy. It will have receded even further from achieving the unattained goal of political equality among American citizens.

Suppose, however, that the United States follows a different scenario: democracy is greatly strengthened, and the power of ordinary Americans over the decisions of their government increases to a new historical level that is well above the upper threshold in Table 6.1. What should we then call our system?

While the problem may seem trivial, without suitable names we are easily drawn into a drastic oversimplification in which we place regimes into two catch-all categories. "democratic" and "nondemocratic," the one "good" and the other simply "bad" or "evil."

WHY AMERICANS MIGHT GROW MORE UNEQUAL IN THEIR INFLUENCE OVER GOVERNMENT

Let me now return to the first of our two scenarios: *political inequality greatly increases* among Americans.[3] To see why this might happen, consider the six barriers to equality that I described in Chapter 5:

1. The distribution of political resources, skills, and incentives.
2. Irreducible limits on time.
3. The size of political systems.
4. The prevalence of market economies.
5. The existence of international systems that may be important but are not democratic.
6. The inevitability of severe crises.

Let's assume that time continues to enforce its implacable limits pretty much as it does now. Each of the other five barriers, however, may actually grow higher and thus generate further political inequalities among American citizens.

THE DISTRIBUTION OF
POLITICAL RESOURCES

In 2005, an article in the *Economist* on "Meritocracy in America"[4] observed that among Americans "[i]ncome inequality is growing to levels not seen since the Gilded Age, around the 1880s." In 1979 the average income of the top 1 percent was 133 times greater that of the bottom 20 percent; in 2000 it was 189 times greater. The compensation of the top 100 chief executives had risen in thirty years from 39 times the pay of the average worker to over 1,000 times. Social mobility had also declined. According to one study,

"The biggest increase in mobility had been at the top of society." And despite widespread American beliefs to the contrary, the evidence strongly supports the view that in the United States social mobility is no greater than in many European countries—and may, indeed, be less. "The United States," the authors conclude, "risks calcifying into a European style class-based society."

As numerous studies have shown, inequalities in income and wealth are likely to produce other inequalities.[5] In education, for example, the *Economist* noted that "[u]pward mobility is increasingly determined by competition," and "[t]he education system is increasingly stratified by class" with poor children particularly disadvantaged (figure 6.2). And, central to our concern here, economic inequalities help to produce political inequality. For example, as Larry Bartels has shown, across a wide variety of issues U.S. senators are far more responsive to the preferences of their rich constituents than to those of their poor constituents.[6]

The unequal accumulation of political resources points to an ominous possibility: political inequalities may be ratcheted up, so to speak, to a level from which they cannot be ratcheted down. The cumulative advantages in power, influence, and authority of the more privileged strata may become so great that even if less privileged Americans compose

Figure 6.2. Income and educational inequalities (2002 United Nations development indicators). Numbers on the left represent the 2002 Global Information Networking Institute (GINI) Income Inequality Index (represented by bars); numbers on the right represent the percentage of people lacking functional literacy skills (ages 16–65) (represented by solid line).

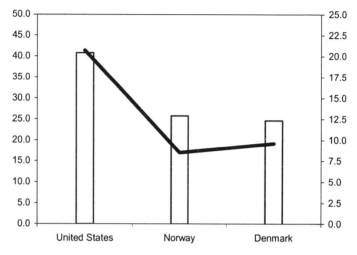

a majority of citizens they are simply unable, and perhaps even unwilling, to make the effort it would require to overcome the forces of inequality arrayed against them,

This pessimistic scenario gains additional plausibility if we assume that for most American citizens the amount of time they have available, or are prepared to make available at the cost of other activities, will remain about the same as in the past. The costs of political struggle might then become so high that too few American citizens would be willing to bear the sacrifices in time and other resources that would be necessary to overcome the superior resources of those in the upper strata, who will more readily act to protect their privileged positions.

Many Americans no doubt view the costs of spending time and effort to reduce inequalities in political resources as too high precisely because *they view the benefits as low or nonexistent.* The absence of perceived benefits to be gained from reducing inequalities in the distribution resources may be more important to them than the relatively high costs of political struggle. In short, the costs of struggle exceed the gains.

Their view of costs and gains is greatly supported by cultural norms. It is a major historic irony that while Marx may have considerably exaggerated the influence of economic structures on culture, systems of market capitalism do seem to foster a "consumerist" culture that greatly weakens any potential opposition to capitalism and correspondingly strengthens its advocates.

Let me explain.

Innumerable studies have shown that among people at the lowest levels of income, increases in income and consumption unquestionably improve human well-being in a great variety of important ways. But innumerable studies have also shown that above a rather modest level, increasing income does not produce greater "happiness" or satisfaction with the quality of one's life. (I'll return to this point in the next chapter.) Why, then, in countries that are exceedingly wealthy by all historic and contemporary standards, do most people continue to find gratification in ever "higher" levels of income, expenditures, and consumption long after their basic needs are met?

In describing what drives persons who struggle for greater political equality, contrary to the views of many philosophers who have given excessive weight to the role of human reason, I suggested that a broad range of human feelings and emotions come into play. Among these are feelings of envy or unfairness when we compare ourselves with others and observe that, for no justifiable reason, others are doing better than us. The "others" are, of course, *relevant* others: persons who, for whatever reason, are viewed as relevant to ourselves—like the capuchin monkeys in neighboring cages, siblings at a meal, the neighbors down the street, a superior at work, or perhaps even a fictitious person appearing in an advertisement with whom the reader can identify.

Examples of the powerful role that envy plays in strengthening the culture and practice of competitive consumption are everywhere. Using just six words to describe "The New 2006 E350," Mercedes-Benz makes its appeal explicit in a full-page advertisement: "More HORSES. Bigger ENGINE. Increased ENVY."[7] Or consider this description of families who relocate to "better" neighborhoods—"relos," as the *New York Times* calls them: "Today's relos are the successors of itinerant white-collar pioneers of the 1960s. They are a part of a larger development that researchers are finding: an increasing economic segregation. [R]elos have segregated themselves, less by the old barriers of race, religion and national origin than by age, family status, education, and, especially, income. Families with incomes of $100,000 head for subdivisions built entirely of $300,000 houses; those earning $200,000 trade up to subdivisions of $500,000 houses."[8]

Paraphrasing Mercedes-Benz, the motto of the consumerist culture might be: "More things, more expensive things, more things for others to envy." Americans in the grip of their consumerist culture are pushed ever onward—ever higher, as they would view it—by their envy of those on the next step upward on the ever-ascending staircase to higher status. And except for the infinitesimally small group at the very top, and perhaps not even them, there is always another group to envy standing one level higher. One of the more recent wealthy residents of Nantucket Island provides this description:

The old money guy has a twin-prop airplane and that is pretty incredible. . . . For his time, that is pretty great. Now he is talking to a guy who is half his age who has a transcontinental jet. That is the end of the conversation.

Or you meet someone and they start telling you about their boat. He has a 45-foot boat and is very happy with it. Then he'll say, "Do you have a boat?" And you say, "Yes." And he says, "How big is it?" That's how people rank them. So I have to say, "It's 200 feet." It's the end of the conversation. Is there envy? Yes, could be. Was he a wealthy guy in his day? Absolutely, but relative to today—no. The two worlds can mix as long as they don't talk too much."[9]

The culture of consumerism exerts far more influence on the thinking and behavior of Americans than what I'll call *a culture of citizenship*. From Aristotle on, philosophers have viewed an ideal political society as one in which citizens actively engage with others in the pursuit of the "common good of all." In a more prosaic and less demanding view, Americans would continue to disagree about what constitutes their "common good," but a culture of citizenship would stimulate a critical mass of citizens to place a much higher value on engaging in political life as a means for achieving their goals. Among these goals would be a reduction in some of the existing barriers to greater political equality.

Yet as long as Americans remain under the sway of the dominant culture of consumerism, even this modest achievement will remain beyond reach.

THE DILEMMA OF SIZE REQUIRES UNDEMOCRATIC INTERNATIONAL SYSTEMS

Policy-makers in nominally independent democratic countries will steadily confront the dilemma of size. They will be faced with problems that impinge to an important extent on their own people but extend beyond the boundaries of their own countries: security, trade, finance, labor standards, health, immigration, poverty, hunger, human rights violations, and many others. To grapple with problems like these, policy-makers will often choose to sacrifice more of their country's autonomy by entering into international treaties, organizations, alliances, and other associations.

Large and powerful as it may be, the United States is not and will not be immune to these challenges. It seems highly plausible, then, to conclude that the importance and influence of international organizations will continue to grow. With the possible exception of the European Union (to which the United States does not belong), the internal governments of international organizations will not be democratic. Instead, as I pointed out in the previous chapter, they will be governed by bureaucracies that will arrive at their decisions through hierarchies and bargaining among the bureaucratic leaders themselves. Even if the American government manages somehow to hold the governments of international organizations accountable for acting within their proper spheres—which will not be easy—American citizens will play a pitifully small direct or indirect role in the process.

To avoid misunderstanding, let me restate that international organizations are not only inevitable; the dilemma of size means that they are often also desirable for attaining ends that Americans favor. Even so, the gains to Americans from participating in international organizations will be achieved at the cost of greater political inequality between most American citizens and their bureaucratic and political leaders.

TERRORISM

As I pointed out in Chapter 4, in democratic countries (perhaps, indeed, in nondemocratic countries as well) a crisis generally favors a shift of control over crucial decisions to the executive branch of the government. Probably the greatest shifts occur as a by-product of international crises like war and, more recently in American experience, dramatic and damaging foreign terrorism. It seems to me no great exaggeration to say that for several years following the attacks of September 11, 2001, ordinary American citizens exercised virtually no influence over the specific actions taken by the American government in response to these attacks, beyond showing their approval and thus conferring a measure of "democratic" legitimacy on presidential decisions. The frailty of citizen control was perhaps nowhere more evident than on the decision to invade Iraq. Except to give their tacit approval, ordinary American citizens exercised virtually no influence over the specific actions taken by the American government in response to the attacks of September 11, 2001.

What is more, based on information supplied by the president and his top officials that proved to be not merely misleading but actually false, the citizens' elected representatives in Congress participated mainly by swiftly yielding the president a pro forma endorsement of his proposed actions. The insistent assertion by the president and his officials that Iraq possessed weapons of mass destruction persuaded the Congress as well as the public to endorse the president's decision. Subsequent congressional controls over decisions by the president and his top officials hardly went beyond passive ratification. In short, as the president and other members of the executive branch exercised almost exclusive influence over "the war on terror," political equality among Americans receded, at least on that crucial issue, to a markedly lower level. Indeed, it would be no great exaggeration to say that *in this domain* the president's power approached that of rulers in some openly nondemocratic regimes.

Subsequently the threat of terrorism was employed by the

president and his associates to establish systems of surveillance, control, and arrest of citizens and noncitizens that eroded previously upheld rights and liberties. Here, too, congressional controls consisted largely of ratifying the president's decisions.

A recurrence of terrorism in the United States might well generate a further shift of power, influence, and authority to the president; a diminution in the already minimal role of Congress; and, through presidential appointments to the Supreme Court and other federal courts, a weakening of judicial checks on executive decisions. Because of a decline in the direct influence of citizens over crucial governmental decisions, and also in the influence of their elected representatives, political inequality might reach levels at which the American political system dropped well below the threshold for democracy broadly accepted at the opening of the twenty-first century.

THE MYTH OF THE MANDATE

The likelihood that terrorism will shift power, influence, and authority toward the president is increased by the myth that "the American people" confer on the victor in a presidential election a "mandate" to bring about the policies he had espoused during the campaign.[10] To the extent that the voters and members of Congress accept a presidential claim to a "mandate from the American people," the president's policies acquire extra legitimacy. After all, shouldn't the will of the majority prevail? And if the majority has given the president a "mandate," isn't it entirely proper, indeed obligatory, for Congress to adopt his policies?

The claim to a "mandate" persists even though it rests on two wholly dubious assumptions.

- Although the claim of a presidential mandate (if not the word itself) can be traced as far back as Andrew Jackson, the absence of scientific opinion surveys makes any such claim before 1940 wholly implausible. The only reliable information provided by the outcome of an election is the number of votes cast for the winning and losing candidates. Without scientific surveys of a large random sample of voters who are representative of all voters, how could anyone know what a majority of voters *intended* as they cast their ballots? Even the introduction of scientific opinion surveys in 1940 has not satisfactorily solved the problem. To be sure, large random samples can provide a fairly high degree of accuracy about the distribution of opinions among citizens as a whole. But if the pollster's questions are not preceded by thoughtful *deliberation* on the part of the respondents, the answers will be no more than shallow responses, not necessarily what voters might actually support if they had an opportunity to acquire more information, more time to reflect on the implications of the proposed policy, and an opportunity to discuss it with their fellow citizens and independent experts.

- Claims for a mandate suffer from a second serious defect. Because of the votes cast for third-party candidates and the vagaries of the electoral college, in about one election out of three the presidency has been won by a candidate who received less than a majority of votes. If the second choices of those who voted for third-party candidates had been counted, the loser might well have turned into the winner—and no doubt the new winner would now have claimed a "mandate" for *his* policies. In 1960, although John F. Kennedy received less than 50 percent of the popular vote, "on the day after the election, and every day thereafter, he rejected the argument that the country had given him no mandate. Every election has a winner and a loser, he said in effect. There may be difficulties with Congress, but a margin of only one vote would still be a mandate."[11] In 2,000, Al Gore gained 48.41 percent of the popular vote, while George W. Bush, the winner in the electoral college, received only 47.89 percent. Moreover, a substantial majority of voters who cast their ballots for third-party candidates would probably have preferred Gore to Bush. None of this inhibited Bush's supporters from claiming a "mandate" for his policies, several of which, such as the elimination of inheritance taxes, he managed to push through a compliant Congress.[12]

Although the "mandate" produced by elections is a myth, belief in that myth greatly enhances the authority and influence of an American president, particularly in times of crisis.

CHAPTER 7

Why Political Inequality May Decline

A lthough something along the lines of the pessi-mistic scenario I have sketched in the last chap-ter seems to me rather likely, for several reasons I would urge us not to assume that this future is inevitable.

First, the extraordinary changes toward political equality over the past several centuries that I mentioned in Chapter 3—not to mention a vast panoply of other changes—counsel us to keep our minds open about future possibilities. How many persons alive in 1700—or, for that matter, in 1800 or 1900—would have foreseen the magnitude of the movement toward greater political equality that would take place by the twenty-first century?

Second, a point I'll return to briefly in a moment, the demise of socialism has certainly not led to the demise of ef-forts and policies intended to reduce the injustices of market capitalism. Following the earlier "welfare state" reforms and, in the United States, the New Deal, the continuing harms of market capitalism have stimulated concerned scholars and others to explore further ways of reducing our unjustifiable social, economic, and political inequalities. The result is a large array of thoughtful proposals, some if which are listed in Table 7.1.

Finally, unforeseen historical events highly contingent on the actions of a very few persons can occur that produce consequences of extraordinary importance: the declarations of war following the assassination of Archduke Ferdinand in 1914, Lenin's arrival in Saint Petersburg from Switzerland in 1917, the appointment of Hitler as German chancellor in late 1932, the terrorist attacks on New York and Washington on September 11, 2001, and many others.

In this final chapter, I am going to explore the possibility that a large but by no means improbable change in American culture and values will help to bring the goal of political equality somewhat closer.[1] Let me emphasize once again that I view this development as only one of many possibilities. A decline in political equality along the lines I sketched in the last chapter may be somewhat more likely. Yet that bleak future is by no means inevitable.

In exploring a more promising scenario, I am going to assume that the danger of terrorism persists through the decades to come, but the threat it poses comes to be viewed as one of the persistent dangers of our lives that we simply learn to endure. Terrorism takes its place among the many

Table 7.1. Reforms to Increase Political Equality in the United States

	Type of Reform	Description	Source
Reforms Addressing Political Equality Directly	Campaign finance reform	Expand McCain-Feingold legislation. Place further limits on corporations, unions, and individual donors' ability to use their wealth to influence politicians. Adopt rules constraining 527 political organizations by making them register with the FEC and abide by contribution limits similar to those of political parties.	A. Corrado and T. Mann, "Flap Over 527s Aside, McCain-Feingold Is Working as Planned," The Brookings Institution, May 2004.
	Electoral reform	Enhance voter/citizen participation. Establish a new nonpartisan agency that will that will set technical standards for voting equipment, gather systematic data on the performance of various election systems, and investigate best practices on all aspects of election administration. A federal grant program should also be established to help state and local governments upgrade all aspects of their election systems (i.e., registration list maintenance, voting machines, poll workers, and voter education).	T. Mann, "An Agenda for Election Reform," The Brookings Institution, June 2001.

Reforms Addressing Political Equality Indirectly (Via Raising Economic and Social Equality)		
Redistricting reform	Reduce partisan and incumbent manipulation of the redistricting process. Persuade congress to adopt additional standards for redistricting by the states. Convince the courts to find gerrymandering plans unconstitutional. Change the process by which states draw legislative maps. Establish independent nonpartisan redistricting commissions.	T. Mann, "Redistricting Reform," The National Voter, June 2005.
Universal health care coverage	Achieving universal health care coverage by building on the Medicare program. Employers either automatically enroll employees in a plan at least as generous as the enhanced Medicare benefits package or pay a modest payroll-based contribution to help fund enrollment of their employees in Medicare Plus. Individuals outside the workforce who are not enrolled by their state would have an individual buy-in option available, with the premium based on income.	J. Hacker, "Medicare Plus Proposal: A Plan for Universal Health Care Coverage." Details of the proposal for Medicare expansion can be found at pantheon.yale.edu/ ~jhacker.

Table 7.1. *Continued*

Type of Reform	Description	Source
Programs to enhance savings among the poor	Improve savings among those households most in danger of inadequately preparing for retirement by expanding/making permanent the Saver's Credit Program enacted in 2001. The Saver's Credit provides a Government-matching contribution (which is higher for those with less income) in the form of a nonrefundable tax credit, for voluntary individual contributions to retirement savings arrangements (i.e., IRA).	W. Gale, J. M. Iwry, and P. Orszag, "The Saver's Credit: Expanding Retirement Savings for Middle-and Lower-Income Americans," Retirement Security Project, March 2005.

| Raise minimum wage, increase the Earned Income Tax Credit (EITC), and expand child care subsidies | Expansion of government programs that increase earnings and encourage full-time work among lower-wage workers. | I. Sawhill, and A. Homas, "A Hand Up for the Bottom Third: Toward a New Agenda for Low-Income Working Families," The Brookings Institution, May 2001. |
| Make higher education accessible to more people | Create a college tax credit or deduction for middle-class families | A. Gore, 2000 Presidential Debates, St. Louis, October 17, 2000. |

Note: I am indebted to Stephen Kaplan for preparing this table.

daily threats to life: 435,000 deaths annually attributed to the use of tobacco, 85,000 from alcohol, 26,000 from motor vehicle crashes, 29,000 involving firearms, 20,000 from homicide, and others. Without minimizing the tragedy of every death, the "war" on terror might begin to take its place in our daily lives along with the "wars" that are regularly declared on tobacco, obesity, alcohol, AIDS, drugs, and the like. In fact, an early sign of a shift in that direction was the change of language among members of the Bush administration in July 2005, when they began to replace the "war on terrorism" with "a global struggle against violent extremism."[2]

WE HAVE THE WAYS. DO WE HAVE THE WILL?

The actions I have listed in Table 7.1 might reduce the unacceptably large political inequalities that exist among American citizens.

As the table illustrates, there are many policies that, if adopted, would help to move us closer to the goal of political equality. The question, then, is not one of *ways*. We have the ways. What we Americans lack is the *will* to undertake these actions.

This leads me to my third reason for hope: It is by no means unlikely that advanced capitalism will foster a revolt against our worship of consumption and our focus on ever-increasing gains for consumers. For a growing number of persons, the goal of consumer satisfaction may yield to the goal of civic participation. The now dominant culture of consumerism may then give way to a culture of citizenship that would promote, among other ends, greater political equality among Americans.

FROM CONSUMERISM TO CITIZENSHIP

Is this simply one more utopian dream doomed to disappointment in the face of reality? Is it like the dreams of socialists and others throughout the nineteenth and much of the twentieth centuries who believed that market capitalism would be displaced, peacefully or through violence, by a socialist system in which the "private" ownership and control of the means of production and distribution would be replaced by some form of "collective" or "social" ownership and control, and the gross inequalities of capitalism would give way to a much greater level of economic, social, and political equality? As I pointed out in Chapter 4, well before the end of the twentieth century these dreams were largely gone as more and more people awoke to the harsh reality that all attempts to replace market capitalism with socialism had failed dismally, not only economically but also, judged from a democratic perspective, politically. To turn Trotsky's famous phrase against its source, socialist programs for replacing market capitalism had fallen into the dustbin of history.

Is this the predestined fate of my suggestion that the culture of consumerism might give way to a culture of citizenship? Several experiences suggest that we should be wary of such a hasty dismissal.

The success of socialism was contingent on the *failure* of market capitalism. The cultural shift from consumerism to citizenship is more likely to come about, not because of the failure of market capitalism, but because of its *success*. Marx predicted that "the contradictions of capitalism" would bring about revolutionary changes in consciousness, culture, society, politics, and the economy. But capitalism rejected his script.

The true contradiction of capitalism is this: its very success in satisfying a powerful human drive toward the ever-increasing consumption of the outputs of capitalist enterprise contradicts another and even more powerful human drive. This is the drive to seek happiness or, if you prefer, a sense of well-being. Numerous studies have shown that once people have achieved a rather modest level of consumption, further increases in income and consumption no longer produce an increase in their sense of well-being or happiness. As more and more people in the rich countries experience this basic aspect of human nature, they will look for more satisfying forms of achievement. In a rich country like the United States, many persons may begin to find that political engagement in some form is more rewarding than spending time, energy, and money on capitalism's ever-expanding output of goods and services. A culture that emphasizes citizenship might then nudge aside the heavy emphasis on the joys of consumerism that is a central part of our prevailing culture. To put it another way, more and more Americans may evolve from avid consumers into active citizens.

WHAT GNP MEASURES— AND WHAT IT DOES NOT

The legitimacy of our prevailing culture of consumerism has been enhanced by a highly influential intellectual perspective in which consumer satisfaction is the measure of economic gain and progress. Let me explain.

Neoclassic economic theory provides a powerful, often useful, and sometimes logically elegant demonstration of the efficiency of a system of market capitalism. Simply put, in this theoretical model, independent business firms compete in free markets for land, labor, and capital to convert into goods and services that they will then sell to consumers in competitive markets. Bypassing troublesome questions of monopoly, oligopoly, unfair trade practices, and other deviations from the model, I want to call attention here to the *centrality of the consumer* in measuring the results of competitive market capitalism. The "value" of a good or service is its value in "satisfying consumer preferences." "Economic efficiency" is measured by the ratio between the "costs" of goods and services used in production, and the "value" of the output produced for the market, where inputs and outputs are measured by their prices in competitive markets.

A country's Gross National Product (GNP), then, is the sum total of its net outputs for consumers, as measured by market prices. A country's GNP per capita is simply its GNP divided by the number of persons in the country. If we remain strictly within the confines of the theoretical model, the higher the GNP per capita, the higher the degree of "consumer satisfaction" among the people of the country. The higher the degree of consumer satisfaction, the better off are the people of that country. It follows, then, that if and as GNP per capita increases in a country, the better off its people are. Likewise, if the per capita income for Americans is higher than that among the Swiss or the Australians, then Americans are better off than Swiss or Australians.

Either this conclusion is nothing more than circular reasoning, or else it is false.

If to be "better off" means, by definition, that consumers have more goods and services available for consumption, then the reasoning is purely circular: to be better off = having more goods, and services available for consumption = to be better off. But if we believe that the quality of our lives depends on more than consumption, and if "quality of life" is interpreted as an empirical statement subject to observation and measurement, then the statement is demonstrably false.

QUALITY OF LIFE

"Quality of life" can be assessed in several ways. Some scales—I'll call them "objective"—combine measures of health, employment, family life, and so on. Others, which I'll call "subjective," are based on judgments made by persons who are drawn in a random sample and whom interviewers ask about their own sense of well-being or the quality of their own lives. Many studies across many countries support these conclusions:

- An increase in income is very likely to result in a great improvement in the quality of life of persons whose incomes are below a relatively low but highly crucial threshold. I'll call this the *quality of life threshold.*
- Consequently, allocating appropriate resources to people who are below the quality of life threshold will, on average, greatly improve their lives, as measured along both objective and subjective scales.

- The average incomes of people in a large number of advanced countries are, however, well above the quality of life threshold (figure 7.1). In sharp contrast to those who are below the quality of life threshold, the quality of life for most people above this threshold does not rise with higher incomes or greater consumption. Thus the great increases in the personal incomes of people in the advanced countries do not appear to have led to higher levels of satisfaction with the quality of their lives. By their own estimates, for example, they are no happier than they were before. As one writer has put it in the *Wall Street Journal*, "Since World War II, Gross Domestic Product (GDP) per capita in the US has tripled, but life satisfaction (measured by surveys that ask something like, 'overall, how satisfied are you with your life?') has barely budged. Japan, too, has had a stupendous rise in GDP per capita since 1958, yet measures of national happiness have been flat. The same holds true for much of Western Europe."[3]

- The failure of increasing GDP per capita to produce an increase in happiness or life satisfaction also reveals itself in comparisons among countries at the highest levels. Despite a higher GNP per capita, by objective measures the quality of life among Americans is no higher than it is among the people of many other advanced democratic countries. By some measures it is actually lower. A study

Figure 7.1. High-income countries well above the quality of life threshold (2005 *Economist* worldwide quality of life survey). Dollar figure on the left represents average GDP per person in U.S. dollars. Numbers on right represent quality of life score (represented by solid line).

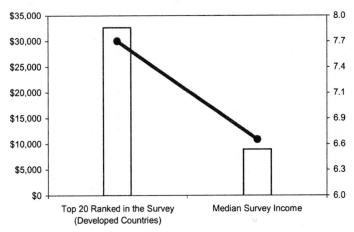

drawing on life-satisfaction surveys for a large number of countries found that while "(t)he main factor is income, . . . other things are also important: health, freedom, unemployment, family life, climate, political stability and security, gender equality, and family and community life." Applying a measure based on these qualities, the study ranked over a hundred countries. Not surprisingly the richer countries topped the list. But among the rich countries, the United States ranked thirteenth, behind Ireland, Switzerland, Norway, Sweden, and eight others (Table 7.2).[4]

Table 7.2. 2005 Worldwide Quality of Life Index

| | Quality of Life | | GDP Per Person | |
	Score	Rank	US$ (purchasing power parity)	Rank
Ireland	8.333	1	$36,790	4
Switzerland	8.068	2	$33,580	7
Norway	8.051	3	$39,590	3
Luxembourg	8.015	4	$54,690	1
Sweden	7.937	5	$30,590	19
Australia	7.925	6	$31,010	14
Iceland	7.911	7	$33,560	8
Italy	7.810	8	$27,960	23
Denmark	7.796	9	$32,490	10
Spain	7.727	10	$25,370	24
Singapore	7.719	11	$32,530	9
Finland	7.618	12	$29,650	20
United States	7.615	13	$41,529	2
Canada	7.599	14	$34,150	5
New Zealand	7.436	15	$25,110	25
Netherlands	7.433	16	$30,920	15
Japan	7.392	17	$30,750	16
Hong Kong	7.347	18	$31,660	11
Portugal	7.307	19	$19,530	31
Austria	7.268	20	$31,420	12

Source: The Economist, *Pocket World in Figures, 2005 Edition* (London: Profile Books, 2005), 30.

A major error in the equation "higher income = greater happiness" is the self-defeating role of status anxiety. Many Americans interpret the equation to mean "higher income = higher levels of conspicuous consumption = higher status = greater happiness." But a substantial body of research shows that this equation is also false. Although not infinite, the status ladder has innumerable rungs, each one higher than the last. A person who takes a step higher soon looks upward and sees persons of conspicuously greater income, wealth, and status.

Given the impressive evidence to support these propositions, it seems altogether possible, even rather likely, that more and more Americans will come to agree with the old dictum that (above a minimum threshold which we have long surpassed) "money doesn't buy happiness."

But if money doesn't buy happiness, where will Americans find satisfaction in their lives? Might not they begin to question the prevalent culture that heavily emphasizes how much people can expect to gain by endlessly increasing their consumption of the unending array of goods and services provided by market capitalism? Might not an increasing number of Americans discover the satisfactions they can gain from working with others to discover and secure the adoption of solutions that actually enhance the quality of life not only of Americans but the millions living outside American borders? In this way might not a culture of consumerism give way a culture of citizenship?

EARLIER MOVEMENTS AGAINST THE DOMINANT CULTURE

In considering these questions it is helpful to reflect on the rise and decline of several earlier movements in which young Americans, drawn mainly from the privileged strata, came to oppose the culture and values that seemed to weigh so heavily in the lives of their parents and predecessors. Two such movements in the United States during the 1960s and 1970s engaged only a minority of affluent youth, and they soon declined, leaving the dominant consumerist culture intact, perhaps even strengthened.

THE COUNTERCULTURE

One was the "Counterculture," which has been described as "various alternatives to mainstream values and behaviors that became popular in the 1960s, including experimentation with psychedelic drugs, communal living, a return to the land, Asian religions, and experimental art."[5] Young people, often referred to as "hipsters" or "hippies," and drawn mainly from middle or upper socioeconomic strata, turned against the surrounding culture of capitalism, work, income, and career, and chose instead to pursue a lifestyle that, by prevailing standards, often carried hedonism and indulgence to extremes. Some aspects of the Counterculture might be understood as a dedication to forms of consumption that were in stark contrast to those accepted in the dominant culture. For members of the Counterculture, the consumer goods they desired were sex, drugs, leisure, and the fellowship of others in pursuit of similar goals, sometimes in communes, sometimes in neighborhoods like Haight-Ashbury in San Francisco.

Many young members of the Counterculture were not so much in revolt against the perceived injustices of market capitalism as they were simply indifferent to them, and chose to pursue their own pleasures without much concern for all those who were outside their own circles. Viewed in this perspective the Counterculture might be seen as the epitome of the egoistic consumer whose satisfaction is the very measure of the achievements provided by market capitalism (even if some of their important markets were illegal).

For many in the Counterculture, however, their pursuit of immediate gratification proved not to be fully satisfying, and sometimes even self-destructive. And as the Counterculture declined in popularity among the young, it left behind little or no change in the structures of market capitalism, the prevailing consumerist culture, the state of American politics and public policy, and the continuing existence of extensive social, economic, and political inequalities.

The Counterculture did reveal, however, that those who are in the strongest position to benefit from the prevailing culture may reject it in search of an alternative that, they believe, will more fully satisfy their deeply felt needs and desires.

PEACEFUL REVOLUTIONARY CHANGE

Much more relevant to my purposes here were the attempts among young persons drawn from the more privileged sectors of American society to bring about a peaceful revolution that would replace the systems that had, in their view, produced huge and unjustifiable inequalities among Americans with economic, social, and political associations that would be far more democratic and egalitarian.

The most prominent of these was the political movement that called itself Students for a Democratic Society (SDS). *The Agenda for a Generation* contained in the "Port Huron Statement" issued by the SDS in 1962 is still worth examining as a set of proposals for a peaceful change toward a more just and more democratic society.[6] Its authors, the former California State Senator Tom Hayden, Gary Wills, E. J. Dionne, and others who would later become prominent in American public and intellectual life, began by noting that they came not from the poor but from the privileged classes.

"We are the people of this generation," the Statement begins, "bred in at least modest comfort, housed now in universities, looking uncomfortably on the world we inherit."

In some fifty pages the authors offered a detailed critique of existing American society and politics, and a set of proposals for the future. The spirit of the proposals reflected their judgment that "[l]oneliness, estrangement, isolation describe the vast distance between man and man today. * * * As a social system we seek the establishment of a democracy of individual participation. * * * We are subject to a remote control economy, which excludes the mass of individual 'units'—the people—from basic decisions affecting the nature and organization of work, rewards, and opportunities."

In contrast to the existing American political and economic systems, politics and economics should be governed by forms of "participatory democracy." For example, "simple government 'regulation,' if achieved, would be inadequate without worker participation in management decision-making." Although the Port Huron Statement did not provide a full portrayal of what "participatory democracy" would entail, many followers of SDS interpreted it as a comprehensive solution for the ills of American life. Systems based on hierarchical authority, and to a great extent even representative democracy, would be widely replaced by associations governed directly by their members: communes, consumer cooperatives, worker-owned-and-controlled business firms, educational institutions governed by assemblies in which students (and perhaps white- and blue-collar employees) participated equally with teachers and administrators, and the like.

The solution of participatory democracy not only ran into strong opposition from those already holding positions of power, influence, and authority. It also faced many of the deeply entrenched obstacles to political equality that I have described. Among these, two were particularly relevant: the costs in time required for participation and the limits on the feasible size of systems that would permit them to be directly governed by assemblies of all the members. The prominence given to participatory democracy as an agent for change probably contributed strongly to the gradual demise of the movement.

FROM CONSUMERISM TO CITIZENSHIP?

Although the revolutions sought by the members of the Counterculture, the SDS, and others in the 1960s ended in failure, their emergence in times of affluence and plenty provides evidence for the possibility that more Americans might become aware of an elementary aspect of their human nature: the quality of their lives and their sense of happiness, fulfillment, and well-being do not seem to rise much with their ever-increasing consumption of the goods and services that the economy so abundantly provides. "We are far richer than our grandparents," many Americans may conclude, "but are we happier?"

As more and more Americans reach this conclusion, they may search for other paths. Many may discover that the quality of their own lives can be enhanced by civic action. Civic activists would soon observe—if they had not already done so—that a fundamental premise and promise of democracy, political equality, is steadily rejected by the realities of American political, economic, and social life.

As they discovered that the ways to reduce political inequality among Americans are many, they would bring to American political life what had been greatly missing: a stronger popular commitment to spend time and energy in order to secure the adoption of such policies.

I have no doubt that, as in every country, full political equality will remain forever beyond the reach of citizens of the United States. As with other ethical ends and goals against which we measure our strivings, our actions, and our achievements, to achieve complete political equality among citizens sets a standard beyond the limits of our human capacities.

Yet as more Americans discover the hollowness inherent in our culture of competitive consumerism and the rewards and challenges of active and engaged citizenship, they might well begin to move the United States considerably closer to that distant and elusive goal.

APPENDIX:
DEFINITION OF POLYARCHY SCORES
...

NUMBER OF COUNTRIES RANKED ON DEGREE OF DEMOCRACY

Score	Brief Interpretation
1	Meaningful fair elections are held, there is full freedom for political organization and expression, and there is some preferential presentation of official views in the media.
2	Meaningful fair elections are held and there is full freedom for political organization, but some public dissent is suppressed and there is preferential presentation of official views in the media.
3	Meaningful fair elections are held, but some independent political organizations are banned, some public dissent is suppressed, and there is preferential presentation of official views in the media.
4	Elections are marred by fraud or coercion, some independent political organizations are banned, some public dissent is suppressed, and there is preferential presentation of official views in the media.
5	No meaningful elections are held, some independent political organizations are banned, some public dissent is suppressed, and there is preferential presentation of official views in the media.
6	No meaningful elections are held, only nonpolitical organizations are allowed to be independent, some public dissent is suppressed, and there is preferential presentation of official views in the media.

Score	Brief Interpretation
7	No meaningful elections are held, only nonpolitical organizations are allowed to be independent, some public dissent is suppressed, and alternatives to the official media are very limited.
8	No meaningful elections are held, all organizations are banned or controlled by the government or official party, all public dissent is suppressed, and alternatives to the official media are very limited.
9	No meaningful elections are held, all organizations are banned or controlled by the government or official party, some public dissent is suppressed, and there is no public alternative to official information.
10	No meaningful elections are held, all organizations are banned or controlled by the government or official party, all public dissent is suppressed, and there is no public alternative to official information.

NOTES
...

CHAPTER 1. INTRODUCTION

1. Specifically, *Democracy and Its Critics* (New Haven: Yale University Press, 1989), 30–33, 83–134; *On Democracy* (New Haven: Yale University Press, 1998), Chs. 4–7: 35–80; and *How Democratic Is the American Constitution?* (New Haven: Yale University Press, 2001), 130–139.

CHAPTER 2. IS POLITICAL EQUALITY A REASONABLE GOAL?

1. Here and elsewhere I have drawn on Stanley I. Benn, "Egalitarianism and the Equal Consideration of Interests," in J. R. Pennock and J. W. Chapman, *Equality (Nomos IX)* (New York: Atherton Press, 1967), 61–78.

2. In *The Wisdom of Crowds* (New York: Doubleday, 2004), James Surowiecki begins his account with the distinguished scientist Francis Galton. "Breeding mattered to Galton because he believed that only a very few people had the characteristics necessary to keep societies healthy. He had devoted much of his career to measuring those characteristics, in fact, in order to prove that the vast majority of people did not have them . . . As he walked through the [International Exhibition of 1884] . . . Galton came across a weight-judging competition. A fat ox had been selected and placed on display, and members of a gathering crowd were lining up to place wagers on the weight of the ox. . . . Eight hundred people tried their luck. They were a diverse lot." When the contest was over, Galton ran a series of statistical tests on their estimates and discovered that the mean estimate of the contestants was 1,197 pounds. The actual weight was 1,198. Galton wrote later: "The result seems more

creditable to the trustworthiness of a democratic judgment than might have been expected" (xii–xiii). In the following pages Surowiecki provides a wealth of evidence to support his belief that, given the appropriate opportunities, groups can arrive at sensible decisions.

3. Max Weber, *The Theory of Social and Economic Organization,* trans. A. M. Henderson and Talcott Parsons (New York: Oxford University Press, 1947), 328–329.

4. See Bernard Manin, *The Principles of Representative Government* (New York: Cambridge University Press, 1997).

5. "When any number of Men have, so consented to make One community or Government, they are thereby presently incorporated, and make one Body Politick, wherein the Majority have a Right to act and concluded the rest." Peter Laslett, ed., *Locke's Two Treatises of Civil Government,*2d ed (Cambridge: Cambridge University Press, 1970), 349. Perhaps no critical analysis has been more influential than that of Kenneth J. Arrow, who in *Social Choice and Individual Values* (New Haven: Yale University Press), 19, demonstrated the possibility of unresolvable cycles in majority voting. For a defense of majority rule see Ian Shapiro, "Three Fallacies Concerning Minorities, Majorities, and Democratic Politics," in *Democracy's Place* (Ithaca: Cornell University Press, 1996), 16–52.

6. Rogers M. Smith, *Civic Ideals, Conflicting Visions of Citizenship in U. S. History* (New Haven: Yale University Press, 1997), 130–131.

7. In 1790, when the first census was taken, out of a total U.S. population of 3.9 million, Negroes numbered 757,000, of whom 698,000 were slaves. In the northern states, with a total population just under 2 million, Negroes numbered 67,000, of whom 40,000 were slaves. *Historical Statistics of the United States, Colonial Times to 1957* (Washington, D.C., 1960), 12– 13 (Series A123–180), 9n.2 (Series A 59070).

8. With the exception of several of his surviving children by his mistress, a slave, Sally Hemings, and her half-brothers. Although the issue of paternity is disputed, Annette Gordon-Reed provides strong circumstantial evidence that Thomas Jefferson fathered Hemings's children. See *Thomas Jefferson and Sally Hemings, An American Controversy* (Charlottesville and London: University of Virginia Press, 1997). For her "Summary

of the Evidence," see 210ff and Appendix B, "The Memoirs of Madison Hemings," 245 ff. DNA tests provide additional circumstantial, though not conclusive evidence. See Dinitia Smith and Nicholas Wade, "DNA Test Finds Evidence of Jefferson Child by Slave," *New York Times,* November 1, 1998.

9. Henry Reeve, trans., vol. 1 (New York: Schocken Books, 1961), lxxxi.

10. I have drawn these estimates from Adrian Karatnycky, "The 1999 Freedom House Survey: A Century of Progress," *Journal of Democracy* 11, no. 1 (January 2000): 187–200; Robert A. Dahl, *Democracy and Its Critics* (New Haven: Yale University Press, 1989), 240, table 17.2; and Tatu Vanhanen, *The Emergence of Democracy, A Comparative Study of 119 States, 1850–1879* (Helsinki: The Finnish Academy of Sciences and Letters, 1984): 120, table 22.

11. For a different formulation, but one fully compatible with what I present here, see Michael Walzer's "emancipation" and "empowerment" models in his *Politics and Passion, Toward a More Egalitarian Liberalism* (New Haven: Yale University Press, 2004), 21–43.

12. *Domination and the Arts of Resistance* (New Haven: Yale University Press, 1990), 117.

13. Because of the greater availability of property, a franchise based on property ownership and set at a fairly modest level enabled a substantial proportion of white males to vote in many of the colonies. Although estimates are uncertain, in at least ten of the thirteen colonies, more than 50 percent of white male adults could vote in elections for local and colonial legislative bodies, and in seven—New Hampshire, Massachusetts, Connecticut, New York, Pennsylvania, South Carolina, and Georgia—the proportion may have reached 80 percent. I have drawn these estimates from Chilton Williamson, *American Suffrage from Property to Democracy, 1760–1860* (Princeton: Princeton University Press, 1960), 3–19. By one estimate, in Britain, the right to vote in parliamentary elections was held to around 5 percent of the population over twenty years old, or perhaps around 10 percent of the male population over twenty; with the Great Reform of 1832, the proportions were increased to 7.1 percent and 14.2 percent, respectively. Dolf Sternberger and Bernhard Vogel,

Die Wahl der Parlamente, vol. 1 (Berlin: Walter de Gruyter, 1969), 632, table 1.

1. Michael Walzer forcefully makes this point in his *Politics and Passion,* 111–130, in which he observes that "the dichotomies that set passionate intensity against some sort of interested or principled rationality, heat against light, are so pervasive in political thinking that perhaps it is enough to say simply that they are useless, that they correspond to nothing in the actual experience of political engagement.... No political party that sets itself against the established hierarchies of power and wealth, no movement for equality or national liberation, for emancipation or empowerment, will ever succeed unless it arouses the affiliative and combative passions of the people at the lower end of the hierarchies. The passions that it arouses are certain to include envy, resentment, and hatred, since these are the common consequences of hierarchical domination.... But anger at injustice and a sense of solidarity are also among the passions aroused by anti-hierarchical politics" (130).

2. *Treatise of Human Nature (1739–40)* (Oxford: Oxford University Press, 2000), p. 415.

3. Translated and analyzed by H. J. Paton (New York: Harper Torchbooks, 1956), 66. For further comments from his *Groundwork of the Metaphysics of Morals,* see p. 57.

4. I confess I find this so profoundly lacking in an understanding of human nature that I cannot help but wonder whether Kant himself was somehow deprived of normal human feelings.

5. Cambridge: Harvard University Press, 1971.

6. For excellent examples with contributions by many distinguished scholars, see Norman Daniels, ed., *Reading Rawls, Critical Studies of a Theory of Justice* (New York: Basic Books, n.d.).

7. Ibid., 46.

8. Ibid., 11.

9. Ibid., 60–61.

CHAPTER 4. A RESPECTABLE ROLE FOR EMOTIONS

1. See further my "Reflections on Human Nature and Politics: From Genes to Political Institutions," in *The Art of Political Leadership*, ed. L. Berman (Rowman and Littlefield, 2006).

2. Sarah F. Brosnan and Frans B. M. De Waal, *Nature* 425 (18 September 2003): 297–299.

3. Nicholas Wade, "Genetic Basis to Fairness, Study Hints," *New York Times*, September 18, 2003.

4. Antonio R. Damasio, *Descartes' Error, Emotion, Reason, and the Human Brain* (New York: Avon Books, 1994).

5. Pages 108–109.

6. Frans De Waal, *Good Natured, The Origins of Right and Wrong in Humans and Other Animals* (Cambridge, MA: Harvard University Press, 1996), 40ff.

7. *James Mill and the Art of Revolution* (New Haven: Yale University Press, 1963), 23–24.

8. See Robert A. Caro's detailed account, *The Years of Lyndon Johnson, Master of the Senate* (New York: Alfred A. Knopf, 2002), 685–1014. His complex racial views are described in Chapter 31, "The Compassion of Lyndon Johnson," 711–739.

9. Because Caro's volume ends with Johnson's election to the vice presidency in 1964, here I am forced to speculate.

10. Pankaj Mishra, "India: The Neglected Majority Wins!" *New York Review*, August 12, 2004, 30–37.

11. "The genetic inheritance of *Homo sapiens sapiens*, which evolved during the 7m years or so that separates us from our common ancestor with chimpanzees and bonobos, equipped man to succeed as a hunter-gatherer. Humans cooperated with each other in hunting and fighting, but this cooperation occurred in groups of close relatives. Human evolution favored caution and mistrust, so far as strangers were concerned. Yet modern man engages in the sharing of tasks and in an extremely elaborate division of labor with strangers—that is, with genetically unrelated members of his species. Other animal (such as bees) divide tasks in a complex

way among members of the group, but the work is kept within the family. Cooperation of a sort among different animal species is also quite common, though not very surprising, since members of different species are generally not competing with one another for food, still less for sexual partners. Elaborate co-operation outside the family, but within the same species, is confined to humans." *The Economist* (August 14, 2004): 69.

CHAPTER 5. POLITICAL EQUALITY, HUMAN NATURE, AND SOCIETY

1. For an excellent description of his skills in influencing the passage of the Civil Rights Acts of 1957, over the opposition of his Democratic Senate colleagues from the South, see Robert A. Caro, *The Master of the Senate* (New York: Alfred A. Knopf, 2002): 944–989, 1004–1005. As president, Johnson later employed his skills to secure the passage of the Civil Rights Act of 1964 and of 1965.

2. Notably Gaetano Mosca, *The Ruling Class* (Elementi di Scienza Politica), ed. and rev. Arthur Livingston (New York: McGraw-Hill: 1939); and C. Wright Mills, *The Power Elite* (New York, 1956). For a critical view, see my "A Critique of the Ruling Elite Model?" *American Political Science Review* 52, no. 2 (June 1958): 462–469.

3. Mogens Herman Hansen, *The Athenian Democracy in the Age of Pericles* (Oxford: Blackwell, 1991), 130.

4. This solution has made it possible for New England town meetings to continue in Vermont, where they appear to meet a comparatively high level of democracy. See Frank M. Bryan, *Real Democracy, The New England Town Meeting and How It Works* (Chicago: University of Chicago Press, 2004).

5. In what follows I have drawn on *On Democracy,* 109ff, and "A Democratic Dilemma: System Effectiveness Versus Citizen Participation," *Political Science Quarterly* (1994): 23–34.

6. To the best of my knowledge, theories of "market socialism" were not advanced until the 1930s. An influential work was Oscar Lange, "On the Economic Theory of Socialism," in *On the Theory of Economic Socialism,* ed. Benjamin E. Lippincott (Minneapolis: 1938): 90–98.

7. Charles E. Lindblom, *The Market System, What It Is, How It Works, and What to Make of It* (New Haven: Yale University Press, 2001).

8. See my "Can International Organizations Be Democratic? A Skeptic's View," in *Democracy's Edges*, ed. Shapiro and Hacker-Gordon (Cambridge University Press, 1999): 19–36; and "Is Postnational Democracy Possible?" in *Nation, Federalism, and Democracy: The EU, Italy, and the American Federal Experience*, ed. Sergio Fabbrini (Bologna: Editrice Compositori), 35– 46. Republished as "Is International Democracy Possible? A Critical View," in *Democracy and Federalism in the European Union and the United States, Exploring Post-National Governance*, ed. Sergio Fabbrini (London: Routledge, 2005), 194–204.

9. See Robert A. Dahl and Charles Lindblom, *Politics, Economics, and Welfare* (New York: Harper and Bros., 1953).

CHAPTER 6. WILL POLITICAL INEQUALITY INCREASE IN
THE UNITED STATES?

1. I am indebted to Michael Coppedge for providing me with the scale scores for Table 6.1. 1. Because all of the countries had representative systems and universal suffrage, these were omitted from the scale as redundant.

2. The full array of categories on which the scale scores are based are shown in the appendix.

3. For a succinct summary of factors fostering political inequality in the United States, see *American Political Science Association Task Force on Inequality and American Democracy, American Democracy in an Age of Rising Inequality* (American Political Science Association, 2004).

4. *The Economist* (January 1, 2005): 22–24.

5. See the ten-part series "Class Matters," in the *New York Times* (May 22, 2005–June 12, 2005).

6. Larry M. Bartels, "Economic Inequality and Political Representation," unpublished manuscript, 2005 (http://www.princeton.edu/7E bartels/economic.pdf).

7. E.g., May 27, 2005, A9.

8. *New York Times,* June 1, 2005, A12.

9. "Old Nantucket Warily Meets the New," *New York Times,* June 5, 2005, 16.

10. See my "Myth of the Presidential Mandate," *Political Science Quarterly* 105, no. 3 (Fall 1990): 355–372; and Stanley Kelley, Jr. *Interpreting Elections* (Princeton: Princeton University Press, 1983).

11. William Safire, quoting Kennedy's aide and confidant Theodore Sorenson, in *Safire's Political Dictionary* (New York: Random House, 1978), 398.

12. In *Death by a Thousand Cuts: The Fight over Taxing Inherited Wealth* (Princeton: Princeton University Press, 2005), Michael J. Graetz and Ian Shapiro carefully reconstruct the ways in which the presidential coalition led by George Bush favoring the abolition of the "death tax" steadily outmaneuvered its Democratic opponents to again sufficient force in Congress and the public to gain passage for repealing the existing tax on inherited wealth.

CHAPTER 7. WHY POLITICAL INEQUALITY MAY DECLINE

1. For stimulating and influencing my reflections on this possibility, I am deeply indebted to Robert E. Lane. Of direct relevance is his *The Loss of Happiness in Market Democracies* (New Haven: Yale University Press, 2000). In addition I have profited from his extensive research and writing over many years on the subject of happiness, and from our many discussions on the subject, as colleagues and friends.

2. "New Name for 'War on Terror' Reflects Wider U. S. Campaign," *New York Times,* July 26, 2005, A7.

3. Sharon Begley, *Wall Street Journal* (August 23, 2004).

4. The Economist Intelligence Unit, "The World in 2005," http:www.economist.com.

5. *Merriam-Webster's Collegiate Dictionary,* 9th ed.

6. Its commitment to peaceful change was rejected by the Weathermen, a faction advocating violence, who left the organization in 1969.